Y0-BYF-103

Little Black Lies

Thanks for
helping to make
the world a
better
Place.
S.

little
black
LIES

Corporate & Political Spin
in the Global War for Oil

JEFF GAILUS

RMB
Victoria Vancouver Calgary

Rocky Mountain Books
www.rmbooks.com

Library and Archives Canada Cataloguing in Publication

Gailus, Jeff
    Little black lies : corporate and political spin in the global war for oil / Jeff Gailus.

(RMB manifesto series)
Includes bibliographical references.
Issued also in electronic format.
ISBN 978-1-926855-69-1 (HTML).—ISBN 978-1-927330-50-0 (PDF)
ISBN 978-1-926855-68-4 (bound)

    1. Petroleum industry and trade—Environmental aspects. 2. Petroleum industry and trade—Political aspects. 3. Petroleum pipelines—Environmental aspects. 4. Corporate power. 5. Social responsibility of business. I. Title. II. Series: RMB manifesto series

HD9560.5.G34 2012   333.8'232   C2012-903852-0

Printed and bound in Canada

Rocky Mountain Books acknowledges the financial support for its publishing program from the Government of Canada through the Canada Book Fund (CBF) and the province of British Columbia through the British Columbia Arts Council and the Book Publishing Tax Credit.

The interior pages of this book have been produced on 100% post-consumer recycled paper, processed chlorine free and printed with vegetable-based dyes.

For my wife, Ylva, whose unquestioning
love makes all things possible.

For David Schindler, whose tireless
commitment to the truth has
been instrumental in making the
world a safer, healthier place.

And for my parents, Andrea and Fred
Gailus, who taught me to always
speak the truth, no matter what.

Among the calamities of war may be jointly numbered the diminution of the love of truth, by the falsehoods which interest dictates and credulity encourages.

—SAMUEL JOHNSON, *The Idler Magazine,*
November 11, 1758

So let us not talk falsely now, The hour is getting late.

—BOB DYLAN, "All Along the Watchtower"

Contents

Preface   XI

Acknowledgements   XV

What's in a Name?   1

Not All Facts Are Equal   17

God's Work   43

Breaking All the Rules   75

Rethinking Advocacy   107

Key References and Additional Reading   139

Notes   145

Preface

I never planned to write this book. It just forced itself upon me and demanded to be written.

I was on contract with Rocky Mountain Books to write a follow-up to *The Grizzly Manifesto* about wolves when two unexpected events happened. The first was the rather fortuitous recommendation by a friend that I watch Adam Curtis's award-winning BBC series *The Century of the Self.* This eye-opening documentary explores how Sigmund Freud and Edward Bernays used the nascent tenets of psychotherapy to develop a groundbreaking new method of social manipulation. Bernays initially called the method "propaganda" but later renamed it "public relations." Through his early work in political and corporate marketing, Bernays began to realize that the "conscious and intelligent manipulation ... of the masses" was not reserved for totalitarian states; it was also an important part of a democratic society. "Those who manipulate this unseen mechanism of society," he wrote in his 1928 book *Propaganda*, "constitute an invisible government which is the true ruling power" of capitalist democracies like the United States and Canada.

The other surprise was a short essay I read in *Alternatives Journal* by Bob Gibson, an environmental studies professor at the University of Waterloo. Boldly titled "Bullshit," the article referred me to a profound little book I'd never heard of: *On Bullshit*. Written by Princeton professor emeritus Harry Frankfurt in 2005, and all of 4" × 6" in size, the 80-page treatise was an instant hit. It spent 27 weeks on the *New York Times* bestseller list and was translated into 16 languages, including Chinese, Hebrew and Slovene. It even got Frankfurt on *The Daily Show*, the only academic philosopher to battle wits with Jon Stewart.

Despite its droll title, *On Bullshit* is a serious work. Frankfurt, one of the world's most respected moral philosophers, wrote it because he was concerned about the preponderance of bullshit in public discourse. For Frankfurt, the most salient feature of bullshit is its absolute lack of connection with the truth. Liars, by comparison, must know the truth in order to disavow it. A liar "insert[s] a particular falsehood at a specific point in a set or system of beliefs, in order to avoid the consequences of having that point occupied by the truth." Bullshitters, on the other hand, have no interest in an accurate representation of reality. They have an utter "indifference to how things really are."

What really concerned Frankfurt, though, was how *comfortable* we are with the ubiquity of bullshit. More so even than lying, an excessive indulgence in bullshit weakens our habit of seeking out the ways things really are and diminishes – perhaps even eliminates – our respect for truth. A society that cares too little for the value of truth, he argues, will be unable to make well-informed decisions in the public interest and will eventually succumb to its own foolishness. "Bullshit," writes Frankfurt, "is a greater enemy of the truth than lies are."

It was obvious that the *Century of the Self* and *On Bullshit* were related. Frankfurt's ideas on the dangers of bullshit was simply a meditation on the negative social implications of the implementation of Bernays's psycho-marketing strategies. And nowhere was this playing out more radically than in the rhetorical battle over the Athabasca oil sands of Alberta. Much of what Bernays and Frankfurt wrote about was unfolding right before my eyes every day: oil companies and governments were consciously and intelligently manipulating the masses to promote the rapid liquidation of Alberta's bitumen fields, and opponents were doing likewise to try to stop it. The stakes were high: whichever "invisible government" won this battle in the global war for oil would determine what kind of future we were going to leave our grandchildren.

The wolves would have to wait.

—Jeff Gailus,
Missoula, Montana, 2012

Acknowledgements

This section is always the hardest to write, for books, like children, require a village to raise. My wife, Ylva Lekberg, deserves a medal of honour for her patience and emotional support during the two years I spent wrestling with this book. I couldn't have done it without her.

Thanks, too, to the journalists, academics and advocates who helped me shrink an entire library of information into a 30,000-word essay. In particular, I'd like to thank David Schindler for being on constant call, as well as Geoff Dembicki, whose on-the-ground research in his War Over Oil Sands series for *The Tyee* provided important fodder for the arguments made herein.

Don Gorman, my publisher at Rocky Mountain Books, was extraordinarily patient and understanding with this project, which took twice as long to complete than I thought it would. Thank you.

People too numerous to mention helped provide information and vet various sections of this book. You know who you are, so please accept my appreciation.

Lastly, thank you to all the people who work tirelessly to put us on a course toward sustainability in a world that seems so resistant to change. You are the nameless heroes who will never get the credit you deserve, but to whom we all owe a debt of gratitude.

little black lie – *noun*

1 a a subtle manipulation of fact that may appear to be true but is in reality false and/or misleading; often used to justify or oppose the development of Canada's tar sands; **b** the subconscious lies we tell ourselves about the world we live in; often used to justify positions not supported by facts.

What's in a Name?

Even though it is the demise of earthly forests that elicits our concern, we must bear in mind that as culture-dwellers we do not live so much in forests of trees as in forests of words.
—NEIL EVERNDEN, *The Natural Alien*[1]

It is difficult even to know how to begin. The rhetoric in the battle over the future of Alberta's bitumen treasure has become so loaded, the arguments for and against so mendacious and untrustworthy, the language so contested, that it is hard even to know what to call the thing about which I have chosen to write.

No matter what I call it, I will enrage or fail someone. If I use "tar sands," I will be dismissed as an environmental radical by industrialists, conservative politicians and much of Canada's mainstream media; if I choose "oil sands," some will brand me an unthinking apologist – a propagandist – for the oil industry and its political servants. But, perhaps what we choose to call it is less important than how we talk about it and what we should do with it.

Whether we call it oil sands or tar sands, it's fair to say that the extraction of Alberta's bitumen has become the most controversial energy development in the world. And for good reason. I have seen first-hand the pyramids at Giza and many of the world's largest dams, and they all pale in comparison to what is envisioned for northern Alberta. Alberta's bitumen deposits contain 169 billion barrels of recoverable oil, the lion's share of the 174 billion barrels that make Canada the third largest deposit of petroleum on the planet after Saudi Arabia and Venezuela.[2] Approximately 140,000 square kilometres – 20 per cent of Alberta's land base, an area larger than most of the world's countries – is scheduled to be mowed down and dug up over the next century. This buried treasure is worth trillions of dollars at today's oil prices, a prospect that has encouraged companies from all over the world – Abu Dhabi, China, France, Norway, Japan and South Korea – to invest in this granddaddy of all oil plays. At the moment, these corporate giants turn Alberta's bitumen into some 1.7 million barrels of bitumen crude every day (more than half of Canada's total crude oil production), and they are only just warming up.[3] Projects approved to date, dozens of them, could increase production to as much as four million barrels per day, the approximate equivalent of one-third of Saudi Arabia's daily production and nearly twice as much as Venezuela's. Industry forecasts indicate that by 2025, if everything goes according to plan, oil companies will be delivering 4.2 million barrels or more of bitumen crude per day, almost all of it destined to feed the insatiable appetites of the United States and, soon, India and China.

When American oil magnate J. Howard Pew opened the first bitumen mine in northern Alberta in 1967, he was destined to become either a genius or a fool. Pew was the president of Sun Oil and the United States' seventh-richest man. Turning bitumen into oil in the late 1960s was an unprofitable experiment that Canadian governments wanted little to do with, but Pew forged ahead anyway. A prescient entrepreneur, Pew believed easy-to-access light crude would become harder and harder to find. Although Alberta's bitumen deposits were difficult and expensive to extract, he reasoned that they had the potential to provide the United States with an abundant source of oil far into the future. And so he invested $250-million in Sun Oil's bitumen mine – and lost money for years. But he knew, or at least hoped, that bitumen's time would come. He need only toil and wait.

For 35 years, the oil sands industry's engineers and accountants worked in relative obscurity, but such an enormous undertaking could not stay hidden for long. As other companies took up the challenge, and the mines expanded and the tailings ponds spread, a growing chorus of critics began raising the alarm about the potential risks inherent in a precipitous development that seemed to be spiralling out of control. Biologists began lamenting the continued decline of threatened caribou populations more than a decade ago. In 2006 a medical doctor and his patients wondered aloud about the excessive rate of rare and lethal cancers in Fort Chipewyan, a small First Nations community downstream.[4] Four years later, ecologists decried the deaths of 1,600 ducks in the toxic waters of a tailings pond. Environmentalists criticized the project's impact on local watersheds and the global climate, as well as the impacts of new and expanded pipelines needed to move bitumen crude to market. As development exploded and reclamation fell further and further behind, critics realized they would need to dig in and fight what has turned out to be a protracted war that has expanded all over the world.

The battle lines are clearly drawn. On one side is a powerful collaboration between some of the world's largest corporations and the governments of Alberta and Canada, which have aligned themselves together in what can only be described as a modern-day Triple Alliance. These captains of industry and government maintain, with the certainty of a host of evangelical preachers, that they are developing Alberta's enormous bitumen deposits responsibly, sustainably and without undue environmental harm. In the same breath, they routinely downplay the environmental risks and accentuate the putative societal benefits – mostly profits and jobs – while proclaiming their steadfast belief that our economy and security – our very way of life here in North America – depends on the rapid liquidation of Alberta's bitumen.

On the other side of the battlefield is a loose co-alition of individuals and organizations – activists, environmentalists, First Nations and a few vocal scientists – arrayed against the Triple Alliance's superior firepower. Big and small, ad hoc and professional, these guerrilla-style fighters differ in their motivations and goals. Some want tar sands development to stop immediately, while others simply want it managed in the responsible, sus-tainable manner the Triple Alliance has promised. Routinely pilloried in the mainstream press for being extremist Chicken Littles, all are worried that the current state of affairs is untenable – that in this, the age of climate change, extracting and processing bitumen and combusting its end prod-ucts in our vehicles is at least as risky as endless proliferation of nuclear weapons.

Although the war is ultimately about oil, the substance in question is actually bituminous sand, a mixture of sand, clay, water and an extremely viscous form of petroleum called bitumen, which itself contains a noxious combination of sulphur, nitrogen, salts, carcinogens, heavy metals and other toxins. A handful of bituminous sand is the hydrocarbon equivalent of a snowball: each grain of sand is covered by a thin layer of water, all of which is enveloped in the very viscous, tar-like bitumen. In its natural state, the stuff has the consistency of a hockey puck.

The Triple Alliance prefers the term "oil sands," while most opponents use the dirtier-sounding "tar sands." Technically, both terms are inaccurate, but corporate and government generals and the soldiers who do their bidding are rarely concerned with accuracy as they build the vocabulary of metaphors that guide our lives. Language has become both tool and weapon, and with hundreds of billions of dollars in profits and government revenues at stake, the linguistic and ethical gloves have come off in what historians may one day refer to as the Great Bitumen War.

The editorial board of the *New York Times* must have had all this in mind when they decided to use "tar sands" in an April 2, 2011, editorial condemning TransCanada Corporation's Keystone XL pipeline as "unnecessary" and "environmentally risky."[5] The $7-billion Keystone XL, which would ferry bitumen from Alberta to heavy oil refineries on the Gulf Coast of Texas, had become a lightning rod of controversy in the United States. The editors at the *Times* must have considered the matter carefully before choosing what they knew would be a contentious headline that included the T-word.

The *Times*'s diction may have emboldened US President Barack Obama to decide, only four days later, to use "tar" in his first-ever reference to Alberta's bitumen deposits, at a town-hall meeting on energy in Pennsylvania. "These tar sands," he said, "there are some environmental questions about how destructive they are, potentially, what are the dangers there, and we've got to examine all those questions."[6] He too chose the T-word purposefully, perhaps to win points with the environmentalists he has so often disappointed since he moved into the White House in 2009. If so, it worked. Environmentalists quietly celebrated the president's controversial diction as a small victory against the interminable roar of the oil industry's propaganda machine.

Canada's conservative politicians and mainstream media outlets, meanwhile, responded with outrage usually reserved for political scandals and terrorist attacks. The editorial board of the *Calgary Herald*, the leading daily newspaper in what has become the capital city of Canada's oil industry, referred to the term as "an inaccurate description favoured by anti-oil lobbyists." The *National Post*'s Peter Foster, a fierce and vitriolic defender of the oil industry, said the *Times*'s "hatchet-job editorial ... read as if dictated by the [pipeline's] radical environmentalist opponents," and dismissed it as just another example of "hysterical environmentalism."[7] Alberta Premier Ed Stelmach was more tactful. He simply wrote a letter to the *Times* and, staying right on message, voiced his concern over the "erroneous information ... used to describe the Alberta oil sands."[8] Apart from a letter in the *Times* from the president and CEO of TransCanada Corp., Big Oil remained mostly silent, content to let politicians and the mainstream media excoriate those who would oppose its black prize.

Given the reaction to the use of "tar sands" by President Obama and the *New York Times*, you might be forgiven for believing that the term has been foisted upon us by nasty, truth-hating environmentalists – but you'd be wrong. The term has actually been part of the oil industry lexicon for decades, used by geologists and engineers since at least 1939. According to Alberta oil historian David Finch, "everyone called them the tar sands" until the 1960s, and both terms were "used interchangeably until about 10 years ago," when the terminology became politicized.[9]

With the notable exception of the Pembina Institute, an Alberta-based environmental think tank that often collaborates with government and industry staff, critics of the way Alberta's bitumen deposits are being developed use "tar sands" because that is what the resource was called when they entered the debate. The term accentuates the obvious downsides of the endeavour – water pollution, for instance, and the decline of certain wildlife species, not to mention considerable greenhouse gas emissions and the infringement of First Nations' constitutionally protected treaty rights – but it is hardly something environmentalists concocted out of nowhere to give the contested development a bad name.

Even the Alberta Chamber of Resources, an industry lobby group, admits that the term "oil sands" gained popularity in the mid-1990s, when government and industry began an aggressive public relations campaign[10] to improve public perception of the dirty-sounding "tar sands." "Oil sands," you see, conveys a certain usefulness, a natural resource that creates jobs, increases government revenues, enhances energy security and makes investors rich beyond measure. The Canadian Association of Petroleum Producers (CAPP), the oil industry's most powerful lobby organization, went so far as to compare the consistency of oil sands mine tailings to yogurt and that of heavy oil to peanut butter. Compared to "tar," "oil" sounds clean and relatively easy to pump out of the ground, like its distant cousin, light crude. Tar, on the other hand, is dark and heavy, the kind of glop better suited to paving roads or coating dangerous subversives before feathering them and banishing them from society altogether.

If this seems like a meaningless meditation on semantics, consider the tragic story of a mislabelled fish. The so-called Chilean sea bass (*Dissostichus eleginoides*), as it is commonly known in the US, is a pelagic fish that is only partly Chilean and not at all bass.[11] Originally called the Patagonian toothfish, it is actually a member of the family *Nototheniidae*, the cod icefishes, which lurks in the depths of the oceans surrounding Antarctica. Bass, by comparison, are generally thought of as popular freshwater game fish. Though there are a few saltwater species, none are remotely related to *Dissostichus eleginoides,* which is a bug-eyed, big-lipped relic of the ages that is almost identical to the sablefish, or black cod, of the North Pacific. The Patagonian toothfish has been called the "perfect fish" because it produces generous fillets of white, mild-flavoured meat with a firm texture that is almost impossible to overcook. Despite this gastronomical upside, initial efforts to market this now popular staple fell flat. For some reason, "Patagonian toothfish" proved unappealing to consumers and the advertisers who try to satisfy their appetites; until 15 years ago, no one could be convinced to buy it.

That all changed when the Patagonian toothfish became the Chilean sea bass. A creative marketing campaign launched by California fish salesman Lee Lantz changed public perception almost overnight, and the new (if scientifically inaccurate) label turned the Chilean sea bass into the darling of our finest high-end restaurants. It is so popular, in fact, that growing demand has sent the Patagonian toothfish population spiralling into the depths. Bruce Knecht, who wrote an entire book on the fish's plight, describes how commercial overfishing and widespread "fish piracy" of this slow-reproducing cod have depleted the fishery, raising concerns that our desire for its perfect flesh will one day drive it to extinction. "It used to be that more fish were caught in some nearby body of water. Now they're coming from the bottom of the earth," Knecht told Tom Brokaw in an interview on NBC. "As long as people want the fish on their table and there's money to be made, fishermen will deliver."[12]

Netting Patagonian toothfish and digging up Alberta's tar sands have much in common: both are in demand and very controversial, and both have become the focus of well-run public-relations campaigns that will make the difference between market success and unprofitable failure. The Canadian media's attack on the *New York Times*'s "tar sands" editorial indicates just how successful the Triple Alliance has been in its efforts to win the public-relations war in the battle for the oil sands. Just check the headlines in any daily newspaper, where the media prefers the term "oil sands" and in the process helps the Triple Alliance promote its interests and brand its opponents as extremists and heretics. The *Calgary Herald*'s Paula Arab[13] claimed the word "tarsands is inaccurate and pejorative. It has become part of the rhetoric of extremists who are anti-oil and who want to shut down the industry," a term that "aborts the debate before it gets started." She went on to say, pointing a finger at Obama, that "Canada has to engage the world in an informed discussion about the oilsands," adding that it "would help if politicians used the language correctly."

The Canadian Broadcasting Corporation actually has a language policy that mandates the use of "oil sands," claiming it is "more neutral and more accurate because the substance eventually refined from the extracted bitumen is oil."[14] But as journalist Andrew Nikiforuk points out in his award-winning book *Tar Sands: Dirty Oil and the Future of a Continent*, if this was really how we named things, then we'd call tomatoes "ketchup" and trees "lumber." Gold would be fine, of course, for it is a native metal found largely in its pure metallic form, but we would need to start calling wheat "flour" and cows "beef." The reality is that the mainstream media uses "oil sands" because the Triple Alliance has made the "T-word" too controversial – and Big Oil spends a lot of money on advertising.

As any corporate communications consultant worth her $1,000/day rate knows, there is nothing intrinsically correct, neutral or accurate about the term "oil sands." Nor is it a coincidence that media coverage has favoured rich and powerful business interests. The media's preference for "oil sands" is simply the result of the Triple Alliance's crafty political spin and an aggressive, well-funded strategy to brand bitumen development in the brightest possible light, part of a much grander battle plan that relies on a dark web of little black lies to win the day.

Not All Facts Are Equal

The environmental disorder which we face at this time is the result of the discrepancy between man's intentions and his achievements.

—PIERRE DANSEREAU, 1972 Massey Lecture[15]

In 2008, as the cancer scare in Fort Chip was garnering headlines, Alberta Premier Ed Stelmach made a trip to the United States to tell American politicians the "truth" about Alberta's tar sands development, part of the Alberta government's multimillion-dollar "Tell It Like It Is" public-relations campaign. In the face of mounting pressure from environmentalists, and an impromptu visit from blockbuster Hollywood director James Cameron, the Alberta government budgeted more than $10-million over two years to promote the province abroad, in particular to highlight the "responsible, clean and sustainable" development of the tar sands. Pro-Alberta ads were run in both New York City's Times Square and London's Piccadilly Circus, and the government spent more than $50,000 to run an ad in the *Washington Post* – it was really an op-ed the *Post* had refused to print – in support of TransCanada's Keystone XL pipeline.

The emphasis, as always, was on "the facts." Jerry Bellikka, a spokesperson from Premier Stelmach's office, told the CBC, "A lot of the critics out there – people who want to shut down the oilsands – aren't constrained by facts. We felt it was important for us to get out some factual information."[16] The ads were simple, and each tried to address one of the criticisms that had been heaped on the Alberta government over the previous months:

> Biodiversity: Only a fraction of 1% of Alberta's boreal forest has been disturbed by oil sands mining. YES. 7.5 million seedlings planted. And counting. YES.

> Water usage: Oil sands projects require water. YES. Oil sands projects recycle 80 to 95% of water used. YES.

Greenhouse gas emissions: Oil sands projects
produce greenhouse gas emissions. YES. Oil
sands projects produce less than 0.1% of
global greenhouse gas emissions. YES.

Innovative solutions: Meeting consumer
demand for oil. YES. Demanding innovation.
YES.[17]

There are other facts, of course, facts that didn't
make it into the government's ad campaign or
onto its website. Facts such as these:

Biodiversity: Tar sands development will
alter 140,000 square kilometres of wildlife
habitat and will very likely extirpate woodland
caribou herds that are listed as "threatened"
under Alberta's *Wildlife Act* and Canada's
federal *Species at Risk Act*. YES. Thousands
of wolves will be intentionally shot and
poisoned in an ineffectual attempt to save the
caribou from disappearing. YES.

Water: Extracting and upgrading one barrel
of bitumen requires 1.5 to four barrels of

water. Annual water consumption reached 170 million cubic metres in 2011, equivalent to the annual residential use of 1.7 million Canadians. YES. Tar sands mining has created tailings ponds covering 176 square kilometres (an area 50 per cent larger than the city of Vancouver) and containing 830 million cubic metres of toxic slurry full of salt, phenols, benzene, cyanide, heavy metals (such as arsenic) and dozens of other carcinogens. YES. These toxic tailings ponds are estimated to leak as much as 12 million litres a day into the surrounding soil and water. YES. As mines expand production, these tailings ponds are predicted to increase to 250 square kilometres by 2020.[18] YES.

Greenhouse gases: Greenhouse gas emissions for bitumen extraction and upgrading are estimated to be 3.2 to 4.5 times as intensive per barrel as for conventional crude oil produced in Canada or the United States. YES. Tar sands are the fastest growing source of greenhouse gas emissions in Canada, accounting for approximately 6.5 per cent of Canada's total greenhouse gas emissions, and they will double between 2009 and 2020, from 45 million tonnes in 2009 to 92 million tonnes by 2020. YES. Essentially the entire projected increase in Canada's emissions between 2005 and 2020 will come from tar sands operations. YES.[19]

Innovative solutions: There are no meaningful technological solutions to any of these problems. There is no strategy in place to protect caribou herds and the habitat they require. YES. There is no known method of reclaiming tailings ponds. YES. And there is no way to meaningfully reduce greenhouse gas emissions from tar sands production. YES.

The best way to figure out where the truth lies is to conduct high-quality, peer-reviewed, scientific research. To substantiate their claims, Premier Stelmach and his industry allies relied for years on the results of the Regional Aquatics Monitoring Program (RAMP), one of more than a dozen organizations and government agencies monitoring the air, land and water in what has become known as the "oil sands region." Initiated in 1997, RAMP is an "industry-funded, multi-stakeholder environmental monitoring program" that "integrate[s] aquatic monitoring activities across different components of the aquatic environment, different geographical locations and Athabasca oil sands and other developments in the Athabasca oil sands region."[20]

Although the Alberta government refers to RAMP as a multi-stakeholder group, the program is largely dominated by the oil industry. It receives almost all of its funding from companies operating in the oil sands region, including all the big ones: Canadian Natural Resources, Imperial Oil, Petro-Canada, Shell Canada, Suncor Energy, Syncrude Canada and Total E&P Canada. RAMP's ostensible goal is to identify and address the "long-term trends, regional issues and potential cumulative effects related to oil sands and other development."[21] For years, RAMP collected data on climate, hydrology, fish and invertebrate health and water quality, and for years it concluded that tar sands development was having no measurable impact on the regional environment. What pollution it did find was simply explained away as the inevitable product of naturally occurring bitumen deposits rather than industrial development.

"The oil sands are a very unique resource, and oil sands development does bring unique environmental challenges," Premier Stelmach told an audience of US business people and members of Congress. "Alberta's oil sands are concentrated near the earth's surface. Contaminants are picked up naturally, through waterways, and enter the ecosystem.... As a province, we monitor water quality carefully, and to date all of the data shows no long-term effects of water quality from oil sands development."[22]

The federal Minister of Environment at the time, Jim Prentice, made similar claims, staunchly defending Ottawa's monitoring efforts.[23] The Canadian Association of Petroleum Producers and the Oil Sands Developers Group, well-heeled lobbyists for the industry, parroted the same line.[24] One Alberta government bureaucrat even went so far as to claim that by removing the toxic bitumen from the ground, the oil industry was actually improving the health and function of the boreal ecosystem of which bituminous sand has been a part for millions of years.

There are two ways to get bitumen out of the ground. What you see promoted in anti-oil-sands campaigns are the great open-pit mines and the toxic lakes of wastewater that accompany them. Giant excavators strip the land of its forests and wetlands to get at the bitumen beneath them, turning a lush, green ecosystem into an industrialized wasteland that astronauts can see from outer space. Four-hundred-tonne dump trucks the size of houses haul the bitumen-soaked sand to processing plants, where it is bathed with hot water and caustic soda. Open-pit mining operations have already removed some 700 square kilometres of boreal forest, an area the size of the city of Edmonton but only about half of the land already approved for surface mining.[25] If oil sands developers have their way, strip mining will turn 4750 square kilometres of boreal forest into a moonscape reminiscent of the battlefields at Verdun.

Processing bitumen creates large tailings ponds, which are actually small lakes full of toxic wastewater behind berms rising hundreds of feet on either side of the Athabasca River. An average of 1.5 barrels of mine tailings accumulate for every barrel of bitumen produced, which means nearly 200 million litres of tailings are produced daily – enough to fill the Toronto Skydome. Together the ponds already cover a whopping 176 square kilometres and contain 830 million cubic metres of toxic slurry, more than twice the volume of Alberta's Sylvan Lake. As mines expand production, these tailings ponds are predicted to grow to 1.2 billion cubic metres by 2030 and cover more than 250 square kilometres.

But, as the Triple Alliance likes to remind us, the ugly open-pit mines and tailings ponds are a relatively small part of the industry's future. More than 135,000 square kilometres (an area roughly the size of Alabama) has been set aside for what is called in situ extraction.[26] In situ, Latin for "in place," refers to sites where the bitumen is too deep to be scooped up and trucked to factories. Instead, a network of wells are drilled and steam is injected, heating the bitumen so it can simply be pumped to the surface. In an effort to improve the development's public image, tar sands proponents have taken to marketing this less visible form of bitumen extraction as "a new kind of oil." Although in situ extraction sites do not look nearly as foul as the pits and ponds, they are hardly less problematic. In situ extraction boils vast amounts of groundwater with incredible volumes of natural gas to inject steam into bitumen formations deep underground, consuming more water and emitting more greenhouse gases than mining does.

Given the size and pace of industrial development in northern Alberta, it seemed inconceivable to David Schindler that all these mines and tailings ponds and smokestacks were not releasing at least some pollution into the surrounding environment – even if RAMP's monitoring efforts were unable to detect it. Although he is routinely dismissed by the oil industry – and even by members of the mainstream media – as a biased anti-tar-sands activist, Schindler is undisputedly one of the world's most heralded aquatic ecologists. He has conducted research on the environmental impacts of acid rain, phosphates in detergents and other serious environmental problems. Now Killam Memorial Professor of Ecology at the University of Alberta, Schindler founded the federal government's Experimental Lakes Area near Kenora, Ontario, back in 1968, about the same time J. Howard Pew started mining Alberta's bitumen. For 20 years he conducted interdisciplinary research on the effects of phosphates in detergents, acid rain, radioactive elements and climate change on boreal ecosystems, and his work has been widely used to formulate ecologically sound management policy in Canada, the United States and Europe.

Dr. Schindler is a fellow of the Royal Society and an officer of the Order of Canada, and he has been awarded some of the world's highest science and environmental honours, including the first Stockholm Water Prize, in 1991, and the Volvo International Environment Prize in 1998. He is, in other words, one of Canada's most respected scientists, who takes seriously his obligation to ensure that environmental and energy policy is based on sound science, and he has never been afraid to take on government and industry when environmental harm and human health are at stake.

Thirty years ago, Schindler conducted a thorough study of pollution resulting from industrial processes that burned large quantities of hydrocarbons. The report was published by the US National Academy of Sciences in 1981, and "we didn't find a single fossil fuel burner or ore smelter that did not discharge lots of toxins that fell back to the biosphere at various distances, depending on the pollutants' properties. The tar sands burn coke, and they smelt ores at 500°C, and the snow is gray for miles around."[27] It was the same with watershed runoff. Scientists have been publishing research on the effects of watersheds stripped of soil and vegetation since the 1970s, and the findings are clear: new geological substrates exposed to rain and snow yield increased runoff of all of the chemicals in the deposits.

"It's Watershed Science 101," said Schindler. "If the oil sands were as free of pollution as the greenwashers claim, it would be equivalent to an immaculate conception."[28]

Indeed, other evidence has already indicated that things were not as "clean" and "responsible" as government and industry claimed. Environmental groups and First Nations living downstream had been raising the alarm for years. Independent research indicated that tailings ponds were leaking as much as 12 million litres of toxic liquid into the groundwater every day, and research conducted in laboratories indicated that bitumen-contaminated sediments often killed fish eggs. Fish that did survive such toxic wombs were plagued as adults by deformities, lesions and hematomas – the same malformations that First Nations fishers were observing with increasing frequency in adult fish caught downstream from tar sands development. Perhaps most chilling are the high rates of rare cancers in Fort Chip, 300 kilometres downstream from the mines and tailings ponds, cancers known to be associated with toxins derived from hydrocarbon development.[29]

Even the federal government's own scientists were concerned that all might not be as it appeared. When a trio of federal government researchers reviewed RAMP's water monitoring protocols in 2004, they questioned whether the program's experimental design could even detect contamination. RAMP suffered from a "serious problem related to scientific leadership," they concluded, pointing to problems of inconsistent sampling and methodology, as well as the inaccessibility of the data it used to draw its conclusions. In short, the reviewers expressed concern that the methodology RAMP was using to collect data was incapable of determining whether tar sands development was polluting the Athabasca River and its tributaries. Schindler and other scientists knew that little had changed to address these obvious deficiencies over the years, and yet politicians, bureaucrats and the members of RAMP's industry-run monitoring program continued to claim that any pollution in the oil sands region were the result of "natural seepage" from underlying bitumen deposits, not industrial development. Something wasn't quite right, Schindler surmised, and he wanted to find out once and for all what it was.

And so Dr. David Schindler – at 70 and well past the age when most of his colleagues had traded full-time employment for golf clubs and the relative ease of retirement – waded into the murky world of tar sands science to see what he could find. First he raised the hundreds of thousands of dollars needed to conduct the necessary research. Then he put together a small team including mercury expert Erin Kelly and toxicologist Jeff Short, to conduct experiments designed specifically to test the claim that oil sands development was not polluting the land and water in the region. Together they mounted two field expeditions in the region in 2008 – one in the winter, when the ground was covered in snow and ice, and one in midsummer – to see what they could find. They were not surprised by their results.

Schindler, Kelly and their team identified a wide

variety of heavy metals lurking in the snowpack and the Athabasca River, some as far downriver as Fort Chip.[30] Seven of the 13 toxic pollutants studied exceeded federal and Alberta guidelines for protecting fish and aquatic life, some by as much as 30 times. These heavy metals include mercury, arsenic, beryllium, copper, cadmium, lead, nickel, silver, thallium and zinc. All are toxic and considered priority pollutants by the US Environmental Protection Agency. Arsenic is a known human carcinogen, and cadmium can harm kidneys and other organs. Long-term exposure to mercury can harm fetuses and cause many serious problems, including memory loss and tremors. Like mercury, lead is a neurotoxin that can cause blood and brain disorders.

Kelly and Schindler's study also found that tar sands development was polluting the air and water with polycyclic aromatic hydrocarbons, a carcinogenic by-product of upgrading bitumen into synthetic oil. Air pollution within a 50-kilometre radius of upgraders deposited enough bitumen and polycyclic aromatic hydrocarbons over a four-month period to equal a 5,000-barrel oil spill on the Athabasca River watershed every year.[31]

For 13 years, RAMP had failed to see any of it. "This [analysis] is so basic," a frustrated Schindler told me over the phone. "The only thing that's innovative is that [we did it] in the oil sands, and we found what you find downstream of any industrial development that involves hydrocarbons."[32]

Schindler had promised the people of Fort Chip that he would make the long trek to their hometown to deliver the results in person. "Lead's gone up fourfold in six years," he told a packed community hall, where distraught residents told story after story of relatives succumbing to rare and deadly cancers. "The same for arsenic. It's gone up threefold in seven years. We conclude that the oil sands industry is adding substantial amounts of contaminants to the river."[33]

Once Kelly and Schindler's research had been vetted and published in *Proceedings of the National Academy of Sciences*, a prominent peer-reviewed journal, they arranged a press conference in Edmonton. Schindler held the deformed bodies of diseased fish in his huge, weathered hands as he delivered the news.[34] You could hear the denial coming from a million miles away.

RAMP quickly defended itself, claiming that

it too had found elevated levels of toxins in the area that sometimes surpassed thresholds found in legislation and water quality guidelines, but that those results had been dismissed as resulting from "naturally occurring compounds" rather than industrial activity. "The Athabasca River and many of its tributaries in this particular region run through oil sands deposits," said Fred Kuzmic, a Shell biologist and the chair of RAMP's steering committee, at the time. "It's not surprising that we would see these elevated concentrations downstream from oil sands operations, because oil sands operations are operating where these oil sands exist."[35]

Politicians took a similar tack. The federal environment minister at the time, Jim Prentice, initially dismissed Schindler's findings as allegations only and maintained that federal scientists had always told him that contaminants were naturally occurring.[36]

When a media scrum cornered Alberta Minister of Environment Rob Renner, a former florist and the man responsible for ensuring that industrial activity didn't pollute Alberta's air or water, Renner dismissed the evidence out of hand.

Despite the growing body of scientific evidence that put the lie to the Triple Alliance's claims, Renner raised his face to a crowd of TV cameras and repeated the same mantra that government and industry had been chanting for years: "There are compounds in the Athabasca River that are naturally occurring and have been there for thousands of years and will always be there because of the nature of the geology in that area."

"Okay, but there's a study refuting what you've just said," said the impatient voice of a reporter off camera. "The study says that humans *are* causing it. You have nothing to point to that would refute that."

"I don't, uh," stuttered Renner, "I don't believe that's what the study says..."

Schindler, clearly exasperated, told reporters, "It doesn't seem to matter how good a research plan we put together, we're supposed to believe they have a database out there somewhere that refutes everything that we've shown? Well, we have our data out there for public display. Let's see theirs."[37]

Schindler, Kelly and their colleagues were soon vindicated. Their research had drawn the world's attention and put the tar sands industry and the governments charged with regulating it in the spotlight. Soon after the results went public, Schindler got a phone call: could he meet minister Prentice for a quick conference at the Edmonton airport? Both Schindler and Kelly attended and walked Prentice through their research, showing him how they had designed the study and what they had found. Prentice asked Schindler what he should do. "I told him about the idea for an [independent scientific advisory] panel, and he announced it the next day."[38]

The federal government's Oil Sands Advisory Panel was the first of numerous independent reviews of RAMP's monitoring program. The Alberta government, caught with its pants down in the blinding light of public scrutiny, and worried that Ottawa was going to interfere with the province's right to develop the tar sands as it saw fit, quickly announced its own inquiry. Canada's Commissioner of the Environment looked into the matter too, as did the Royal Society, which appointed a panel of its own. They all came to the same conclusion: it would be hard to design a worse monitoring program if you tried. Environmental monitoring of tar sands development was disorganized, under-resourced, secretive and ineffective. There was no way of telling what conditions were like before tar sands development started, and it was all but impossible to figure out how development had affected the region over the last 45 years.

With the writing now on the wall, government and industry ceased their defence of RAMP and turned their efforts instead to the rather more difficult task of damage control. "These ugly truths, long evident to aboriginal elders and many scientists, have sent industry propagandists and government falsifiers back to their rooms for a long Christmas sulk," wrote journalist Andrew Nikiforuk when the federal Oil Sands Advisory Panel released its report just before Christmas 2010. "Yes, Virginia, there is a hell for liars."[39]

The federal government quickly put together a team of independent scientists and gave them 90 days to develop the "world-class" tar sands monitoring program it had been claiming it already had in place. Phase One, a conceptual framework for a new world-class monitoring plan and a detailed water quality monitoring scheme for the Lower Athabasca River, was released in March 2011. A more holistic and integrated plan that includes effective monitoring of not only lakes and rivers but also air, fish, invertebrates and mammals, was released in July. The price tag? Fifty million – two-and-a-half times what is being spent now. The Alberta government released the results of its own Alberta Environmental Monitoring Panel in June 2011, which recommended the establishment of an independent environmental monitoring commission.

In February 2012, six years after the people of Fort Chip voiced their concern about the spate of rare and deadly cancers, a new federal Minister of Environment, Peter Kent, and his Alberta counterpart, Diana McQueen, stood side by side in Edmonton to unveil a new monitoring plan for the oil sands region. It still is not clear who will pay for it, or whether it will be overseen by government or a truly independent commission, but both Kent and McQueen were convinced that the new monitoring system would prove to the world how responsibly they were developing "this critical global resource."[40]

It's hard to decide what to make of the great Canadian tar sands monitoring fiasco, largely because what none of the panel reviews bothered to ask was how, in a developed country with a functioning democracy, the pollution monitoring system of the world's largest and most controversial energy development could be so deficient. It's not like we don't know how to do it. It's not like it hasn't been done elsewhere. In fact, proper monitoring had been carried out in the very same region 10 years before. The *Northern River Basins Study*[41] provided scientifically sound information about the water and aquatic environment of the Peace, Slave and Athabasca basins, which were being put at risk by increasing urban and industrial development (mainly forestry and pulp mills). Schindler points to this study as a model that could have been followed in the tar sands region.

Absent an official independent review, there appear to be three competing theories. Optimists point to confusion as the most plausible answer. Despite the fact that representatives from the tar sands industry sat alongside scientists from the Alberta and federal governments at RAMP, some claim there was uncertainty about who was to monitor what, when and to what ends. Others, including Schindler, believe those overseeing the monitoring program simply lacked the necessary expertise; others are less kind and use the word "incompetence." The more cynical among us suggest it may have been done on purpose; all you need to do is look at who benefited from a monitoring system that was unable to detect pollution. It seems impossible to believe that the Triple Alliance thought it could get away with using a faulty monitoring system, and yet it's not impossible to believe they might try it anyway. Worse things have been done in the name of progress.

However late in coming, the unveiling of a "world-class" monitoring system is a positive step, but there is every reason to be skeptical that it will make much difference in the long term. For one thing, it will take years to implement. The plan calls for everything to be in place in three years, but given these governments' track record in implementing environmental management systems, it could well take longer. It will also take many more years, perhaps a decade, before improved monitoring efforts provide sufficient data – data that should already be available – to draw conclusions about the impact of the exponential growth of the tar sands.

More important is to recognize that a monitoring system is designed only to monitor, not regulate.

If all goes well, dozens of scientists will gather mountains of data on air and water, fish and caribou. Scientists will analyze those data in their labs and on their computers, crunching numbers and computing statistics. Ten years from now they'll publish their peer-reviewed studies, which will tell us how fast caribou populations legally listed as threatened have declined, how much toxic pollution has been released into the Athabasca River (and perhaps whether that pollution is contributing to the cancer rates downstream) and whether technological advancements have reduced overall water use and greenhouse gas emissions. But the data itself and the scientists who provide it will not change a thing unless the government changes the rules in order to mitigate or eliminate the nasty consequences of turning bitumen into oil.

Meanwhile, the Triple Alliance shows no sign of changing anything. Despite universal condemnation of the government's industry-led monitoring program by some of the best independent scientists on the continent,[42] and despite Schindler's peer-reviewed research results, tar sands projects are being approved faster than ever. Incredibly, both the federal and Alberta governments are working on ways to "streamline" the environmental assessment process so they can start digging and drilling even faster. Meanwhile, websites of both government and industry still emphasize the "fact" that water in the tar sands region is being closely monitored, that monitoring stations downstream have not detected any problems, and that whatever surface-water pollution we find is the result of "naturally occurring" bitumen deposits.[43]

God's Work

*Do the rhetoricians appear to you always to speak
with a view to what is best, aiming at this, that
the citizens may be made good as possible by their
discourses? or do they, too, endeavor to gratify the
citizens, and neglecting the public interest for the
sake of their own private advantage, do they treat
the people as children, trying only to gratify them,
without being in the least concerned whether they
shall become better or worse by these means?*

—PLATO, *Gorgias*, c. 380 BCE[44]

The website of the Canadian Association of
Petroleum Producers, the voice of Canada's oil
and gas industry, is under the keen-eyed guidance
of Janet Annesley. Thirty-something, smooth and
smart, Annesley is CAPP's vice-president of communications, the Canadian oil industry's version
of *Thank You for Smoking*'s cigarette-selling Nick

43

Naylor. Apparently, the righteous act of persuasion is a family tradition. Annesley's father spent 30 years as an oil and gas spin doctor and her grandfather finished his long career at the Aluminum Company of Canada in public affairs and government relations. CAPP brought Annesley on board because the oil industry felt it was taking a beating in the high court of public opinion and it needed to start a crusade of its own. When Annesley started at CAPP, one of their board members told her she was "doing God's work now," a belief she happily shared in an interview for *Oilweek* as one of 13 Rising Stars "destined to make their own luck in the Canadian oil and gas industry."[45]

After four quiet decades of doing as it pleased in out-of-sight-out-of-mind northern Alberta, the oil industry realized it had to deal with growing public awareness and concern about the impacts of rapid tar sands development. Annesley was hired to help them reframe the debate. "We were caught flat-footed," she told the *National Post*, Canada's right-leaning, pro-business national newspaper. "The oil-and-gas industry was not being effective in engaging Canadians because it didn't have the ability to connect with them emotionally."[46]

Annesley, who keeps a David Letterman-inspired "Top 10" list of the most outrageous falsehoods about the tar sands, apparently blames the industry's relative failure on two things: its reliance on overly technical, jargony language, and "mean-spirited, one-sided info-tainment cobbled together by agenda-driven environmentalists."[47]

No word whether the industry's problems might have anything to do with inadequate government oversight or the fact that bitumen development may just be too risky and destructive in a world already beset by hydrocarbon-induced environmental degradation.

CAPP is one of more than a dozen well-funded think tanks and industry trade groups that defend and promote rapid bitumen development in Canada. Some of these groups have been around for years, decades even, but many have appeared on the scene only recently, just in time share in the wealth of a multi-million dollar public relations industry funded by an eager oil industry.

The US Chamber of Commerce, a powerful corporate lobby, is one of the largest trade associations in the world. The Chamber describes itself as "the world's largest business federation, representing more than three million businesses and organizations of every size, sector, and region."[48] It used to be a bipartisan outfit that tried to tailor government policy to benefit its members, but since Tom Donohue took over as president and CEO in 1997, it "has become a fully functional part of the partisan Republican machine." The Chamber's 2010 budget was approximately US$200-million, and it spends tens of millions of dollars a year aggressively lobbying government.[49] Although its donors are anonymous, much of its work is on behalf of the oil and gas industry and against efforts to curb greenhouse gas emissions.[50]

The American Petroleum Institute is another of the world's biggest players, busily promoting the interests of the oil and gas industry since 1919. It claims to be a research institute "committed to using the best available scientific, economic and legal analysis to guide and support" its policy positions. It boasts more than 500 oil and gas–company members, including many of the major players in the tar sands: BP, Chevron, ConocoPhillips, Devon Energy, ExxonMobil, Shell, Statoil, Total E&P and TransCanada.[51] Not surprisingly, the API has a keen interest in promoting development of

Alberta's oil sands,[52] and has lobbied actively on behalf of Canada's great bitumen experiment.[53]

CAPP is API's Canadian brother in arms and leads the powerful oil lobby in Canada. Its more than 100 producer members include all the major oil and gas companies, including the tar sands developers that belong to API, as well as Canadian Natural Resources, Canadian Oil Sands, Encana, Husky Energy, Nexen, Suncor, Syncrude, Talisman Energy and numerous smaller companies. Like all think tanks on the left and the right, CAPP is decidedly ideological. "They want to influence public policy and public perception and shape the political climate of the day," says Don Abelson, chair of the political science department at the University of Western Ontario and an expert on think tanks. "They want to change the way we think."[54]

CAPP's website is the cornerstone of its efforts to influence us. Here you will find all the facts and frames CAPP uses to convince us, "through constructive engagement and communication," that the tar sands can be developed "in a safe and environmentally and socially responsible manner." Annesley's colleague Travis Davies, a CAPP public affairs adviser, says the website provides information on the tar sands and those who develop it which he hopes will help to open a *conversation* with the public. I am grateful for the opportunity, for there is much to say about the content on CAPP's website.

Not surprisingly, CAPP's website describes bitumen and the processes to extract it in the most benign terms possible. Its "Environment" page, which covers the issues most difficult for industry to spin, is perhaps the most startling example. It starts out by assuring us that "we understand" the growing concerns people have "about the environmental impacts of the projects currently operating, and the ones planned for the future." CAPP readily admits that "oil sands development has an impact on the environment," and feels "it is essential that people understand what development means, because the issues involved are important to everyone."[55]

So far so good: openness, transparency, honesty. Even a shred of humility. Then the anonymous writers wade into the dominant environmental issues one by one, to make it easy for us to take them in. It's complex, after all, and stepwise simplicity helps. CAPP and its members recognize that tar sands production is energy intensive and that it produces greenhouse gas emissions, which it notes as a "contributing factor" to climate change. They're working on it, we are told, by developing "new technologies to lower these emissions, and capture and store carbon dioxide (CO_2)."[56]

Video is now a popular form of web-based communication, and CAPP's site makes good use of it. In "Canada's Oil Sands – Come see for yourself," Dr. Eddy Isaacs assures us that industry has the GHG issue under control: "We certainly have seen a major reduction in GHG emissions over the last 10 years. The number is around 30 per cent reduction in GHG emissions."[57] Isaacs is the chief executive officer of Alberta Innovates–Energy and Environment Solutions (formerly the Alberta Energy Research Institute), a "dynamic" government-funded corporation that aims, among other things, to be "a catalyst for developing innovative, integrated ways to convert our natural resources into market-ready, environmentally responsible energy."[58] Eric Newall, chancellor emeritus of the University of Alberta and former CEO of Syncrude, adds to Isaacs's technological optimism: "It's technology that's got us where we are today, and it's technology that's going to take us where we need to be tomorrow. We have a very exciting future here with a great, long-term supply of sustainable energy."[59]

The honest and up-front character of CAPP's web-based message has begun to dissipate and things are going downhill fast. CAPP is starting to get pretty loose with the facts and the bullshit is starting to flow like oil from a gushing well. What it fails to mention is that despite the 30 per cent reductions in GHG emissions *per barrel of oil produced*, the tar sands will add significantly to our GHG pollution problem. So much so, in fact, that it will be almost impossible for Canada to meet its rather modest commitment to reduce GHG emissions to 17 per cent below 2005 levels by 2020. This reduction amounts to roughly 2 per cent from 1990 levels, a far cry from the 6 per cent below 1990 levels that Canada committed to when it signed the Kyoto protocol. Even with such a low-ball target, Canada has little chance to meet it, in large part because it is making little effort to do so. "Few federal efforts are underway to reduce these emissions," wrote Johanne Gélinas, Canada's environment commissioner, in 2006. "For its part, the federal government is counting on regulatory and long-term technological solutions," but "it is not leading the way by clearly stating how and to what degree Canada will reduce greenhouse gas emissions when oil and gas production is expected to increase."[60] In fact, shortly before she was fired in 2007, Gélinas had reported that any further growth in bitumen production would likely cancel out national efforts to lower emissions.

Turns out, Gélinas was on to something. According to CAPP's own "How We Are Doing" analysis, greenhouse gas emissions rose 14 per cent between 2009 and 2010, not surprising give the rate at which tar sands operations have expanded. Perhaps more shocking is the fact that GHG emissions intensity, which CAPP and Canada's Conservative politicians are proud to tell us has been decreasing, actually increased 2 per cent over the same period. This means that on a per barrel basis, carbon pollution is going up, not down, a trend that is likely to continue as production shifts from mining to in situ extraction.[61] Even though carbon pollution trends are not necessarily the oil industry's concern – after all, it is playing by the rules, however misguided, that have been set out for it – the least it could do is report the facts correctly. And the facts are that GHG emissions from bitumen production will never decrease but rather rise faster than a Saturn V rocket headed for the moon.

The claim that technology will reduce GHG emissions associated with the bitumen boom is not connected to the truth either. According to David Keith, one of the world's foremost experts on capturing and storing carbon dioxide, it is a pretty well-known fact in industry and engineering circles that carbon capture and storage won't work for most aspects of bitumen extraction and consumption. Despite the fact the Alberta government's greenhouse gas reduction strategy relies almost solely on CCS, and despite the fact it has invested $2-billion in subsidizing industry's attempt to develop this unproven technology, it will do little to reduce the amount of GHG emissions generated by bitumen extraction.

As you have probably noticed, these claims, and many others found on CAPP's websites, have little connection to any thoughtful consideration of the truth. Although they are not overt lies, they are so obviously deficient in factual grounding that they become a kind of "bullshit" that political philosopher Mark Evans, in "The Republic of Bullshit: On the Dumbing-Up of Democracy," calls "rubbish."[62]

I could go on and on, but one more example of the Triple Alliance's lack of concern for the truth will suffice, and it has to do with water. While CAPP acknowledges that both mining and in situ extraction require significant amounts of water, it *emphasizes* the fact that water use per barrel of oil at one facility (Imperial Oil Resources' Cold Lake operation) has been reduced from 3.5 barrels in 1985 to just 0.5 barrels today. This has been accomplished, CAPP points out, by using recycled water for more than 95 per cent of water it requires. What this selective bit of information does not tell you is that while recycling has reduced water use, the much-touted *recycling process creates problems of its own,* increasing concentrations of heavy metals, naphthenic acid and PAHs that make the tailings ponds so deadly toxic. Nor does it mention that despite improved water efficiency, these ominous tailings ponds will likely expand by more than 50 per cent by 2020.

The CAPP website proudly boasts that only approximately "1 per cent of the flow of the Athabasca River is used in production of the oil sands." Bitumen extraction and production removes forever a significant, and potentially lethal (for fish), amount of water from the Athabasca River and watershed, and none of what is used can ever be released back into the water cycle, because it has been so grievously polluted. The CAPP statistic of "1 per cent of the flow of the Athabasca River" is based on *average annual flow*, which is an almost meaningless statistic when managing potential impacts of water withdrawals on river health. What really matters is whether the amount of water withdrawn during the winter months, when river flows are as low as 10 per cent of summer flows, harms fish habitat and puts fish lives and populations at risk. In fact, current and proposed water licences could withdraw *more than 15 per cent* of the Athabasca River's water flow during low-flow periods, which *does* pose a risk to fish habitat and the health of the river's ecosystem. This is especially risky for the lower Athabasca, because climate change has reduced average low flows by 30 per cent over the last 40 years, and a warming planet likely will reduce them further.[63]

By omitting this necessary context, CAPP seems wholly disconnected from any reasonable attempt at getting at the truth. These isolated and cherry-picked "facts" ignore the ecological context in which they must be considered, and they quickly coalesce into what Heather Douglas calls "bullshit of the isolated fact."[64] Douglas, who is Phibbs Professor of Science and Ethics at the University of Puget Sound, maintains that the combination of complex scientific information and the tendency of politicians to utilize spin, results in statements that are not false – and thus not lies – but are nevertheless deeply misleading.

This kind of obfuscation by selection is part of a long-standing tradition adequately documented in critiques of corporate propaganda. *Merchants of Doubt* is perhaps one of the best, though there are many other good ones.[65]

The co-authors of *Merchants of Doubt* are Naomi Oreskes, a professor of history and science studies at the University of California, San Diego, and one of the world's leading science historians; and Erik Conway, a historian of science and technology who received the 2009 NASA History Award for path-breaking contributions to space history. Their work documents the well-funded propaganda campaigns designed to confuse and mislead the public on environmental and public health problems as varied as DDT, tobacco, acid rain, the ozone hole, global warming and Ronald Reagan's Star Wars missile defence scheme.

The goal of these types of campaigns is not to prove beyond a reasonable doubt that, for instance, the tar sands are clean and sustainable or that cigarettes don't cause cancer. Rather, the intent is simply to create enough doubt in the public consciousness to maintain the status quo. According to an anonymous cigarette executive in a now-infamous memo from American tobacco company Brown & Williamson – one of four cigarette manufacturers that eventually agreed to a 25-year, $368-billion settlement for health-related damages associated with smoking – doubt is "the means of establishing a controversy ... if we are successful in establishing a controversy at the public level, there is an opportunity to put across the real facts about smoking and health."[66]

Sounds awfully familiar. On the surface, at least, it appears that the oil industry (and the Alberta government) are using the same kind of subtle manipulation of the facts to convince the public that the potential risks of oil sands development are less than they might really be. This makes the Alberta government's plan to sue tobacco manufacturers for $10-billion to recover healthcare costs somewhat ironic, given that the government is accusing tobacco manufacturers of deceiving Albertans by "falsely denying the health risk of exposure to tobacco products," and then "concocting and perpetuating a fallacious controversy as to whether there was a real health risk."[67]

A poster hangs on an Ottawa street. It shows a good-looking, middle-aged man crouching beside a young conifer that grows in the shadow of a stand of columnar poplar. His steel-grey eyes stare straight into the camera – into the viewer's eyes – and his five o'clock shadow emphasizes his pink lips and chiselled chin. His signature identifies the man as Garrett Brown, of ConocoPhillips, and he radiates deadly seriousness. "WE LEARNED HOW TO RE-ESTABLISH THE FOREST IN YEARS, NOT DECADES," the title boasts in bold white letters. At the bottom: "New ideas are making a difference.

CAPP.CA/oilsands." Another version of the same ad tells us that Garrett Brown "grew up on a farm," and therefore "know[s] what it means to have the land restored." Someone has scotch-taped a white piece of paper on the man's chest, right over his heart. It reads, "MISLEADING."

CAPP distributed this poster and others like it, as well as a slew of similar newspaper ads and television commercials, as part of the oil industry's expensive multi-media advertising campaign to "emotionally" connect with the public just as Janet Annesley wanted. The campaign was the result of a two-year introspection starting in mid-2008, when CAPP hired Peter Sandman, a high-priced risk-communications specialist who charges hundreds of dollars per hour for his services. According to Annesley, Sandman told them: "Guys, you need to listen" to what Canadians want to know about the tar sands and what issues they want addressed.[68]

To find out what Canadians were thinking about this, CAPP commissioned opinion polls, met with government officials and opposition MPs, and sat down with environmental organizations like the David Suzuki Foundation and Ducks Unlimited.

The message from at least one of CAPP's polls seemed clear. In May 2010 an unspecified number of Canadians in various cities were asked to choose one of three answers to the question "Which is the best goal when it comes to the oil sands?" A majority (74 per cent) opted for the choice "to develop the oil sands with an effort to limit the environmental impacts." Only 17 per cent wanted "to stop the development of the oil sands altogether," which was nearly double the 9 per cent who wanted "to focus on maximizing the full economic benefits of the oil sands resource."[69] Similar results have been repeated in numerous polls since. CAPP interpreted respondents' environmental concern to mean that "Canadians want a balanced discussion about energy, the economy and the environment."[70]

It is clear that Canadians want to benefit from the economic opportunities presented by the tar sands, but they have also made it clear that they want it done in a socially and environmentally responsible way. But rather than a more open and honest conversation about the benefits and risks of bitumen development, or a real effort to actually reduce the environmental impacts, CAPP simply decided to distract us from the problems by having people "just like us" tell us exactly what the polls say we want to hear.

In one 30-second television commercial, Syncrude Canada's Steve Gaudet wanders through bucolic woods in an area once occupied by a small strip mine. In a moment of feigned spontaneity reminiscent of Wordsworth or Thoreau, he glances into the trees and says, with feigned glee, "Oh, there's two squirrels chasing each other for a cone over here!" In another commercial, Ron Lewko, wearing safety glasses and a hardhat, tells us he looks after environmental research for Syncrude. "My job is to reclaim the land," he says. "I think we've planted over five million trees and shrubs. Once reclamation started, nature took over and the wetland took off by itself. These bulrushes came in naturally. The willow trees around the lake came in naturally. We've got wildlife in here.... It's just a nice place to be."

Technically, this is not a lie. For Ron, it may be a nice place to be. Small areas of disturbed land have been reclaimed, and the promise of total reclamation is often rolled out as justification for allowing large-scale disturbances to continue until the bitumen is gone. But anyone who has actually been there knows that the reality represented in Steve's and Ron's bucolic fantasy world is totally unconnected to the truth on the ground, making these commercials yet more examples of the bullshit of the isolated fact. Some 700 square kilometres of land has been disturbed by strip mines and tailings ponds since J. Howard Pew dug his first mine, and almost all of it is still an ugly, toxic mess. While industry claims that approximately 10 per cent of that land has been reclaimed,[71] only 104 hectares, or just over 1 square kilometre (~0.15 per cent), has been certified as such by the government. The first small tailings pond was "reclaimed" in 2010, but only because the toxic tailings it contained were transported and stored elsewhere.[72] In fact, there is no proven method of reclaiming tailings ponds, and yet government allows them to expand to oceanic proportions based on the promise of finding an unidentified solution sometime in the distant future.

What we are left with, then, is a *promise of reclamation*. Despite having reclaimed only 0.15 per cent of the disturbed area in the last 40 years, industry is somehow going to clean up after itself even as it continues to transform orders of magnitude more boreal forest into an industrialized moonscape. Both the federal and Alberta governments assure us that every oil sands company must fulfill its legal obligation to reclaim 100 per cent of the land it disturbs.[73] The Mining Association of Canada does them one better, promising that the reclamation of the open-pit mines can be done with the vision of a Group of Seven artist.[74]

Such promises are the kind of "bullshit" Mark Evans refers to as "irretrievable speculation," where the meaning "may be perfectly clear ... but is crucially lacking in any plausible means of verification."[75] There is much to support this contention. For one thing, plants do not grow well in the soil salinity created in the wake of a bitumen mine, and it is all but impossible to reconstruct the complex boreal ecosystem, almost 40 per cent of which is wetlands. Even if it is possible, it will likely prove far too expensive to actually do, and the Alberta government has not bothered to ask the oil companies for enough security to ensure it gets done no matter how much it costs.[76]

Whether or not reclamation is possible, however, is almost moot considering the fact that industry is not required to restore the landscape to the way it was before it was literally shovelled up and dumped into the back of a truck. Instead, companies are legally obligated only to reclaim all disturbed land to an "equivalent land capability," which "means that the ability of the land to support various land uses after conservation and reclamation is similar to the ability that existed prior to an activity being conducted on the land, but that the individual land uses will not necessarily be identical."[77] This may sound good, but it is frighteningly vague, and it does not require industry to invest the time and money into returning the land and its water to its natural state. Instead, at best, the mines will be turned into forested uplands that support forests that might one day, a century or two on, be ready for logging. It's like tearing down the Sistine Chapel to build a ten-storey parking garage.

There is little reason to believe, however, that meaningful reclamation will ever happen. The oil and gas industry's existing reclamation track record is already shameful, and there is little reason to think that northern Alberta, and the people and animals living there, will fare any better. Like other industrial facilities, inactive and abandoned oil and gas wells present an increased risk of soil and groundwater contamination until they are reclaimed. Despite several attempts by provincial regulators to resolve the issue over the last 15 years, the number of inactive and abandoned wells has swelled to more than 107,000, and the numbers grow every year. The number of abandoned wells has almost doubled over the last decade, from 25,000 to 47,000 in 2011, and at least 29,000 of them have been sitting in a state of suspended animation for over a decade, some since the 1960s. An additional 61,500 wells are simply inactive or suspended, rather than abandoned, temporarily sitting unused for periods of a few months to more than a decade.

And things are only getting worse. Alberta Environment reported an average of 13,818 wells drilled annually over the past decade but only an average of 1,728 government cleanup certificates are issued each year. Unless sites have obvious problems, such as soil contamination, there is no provincial government deadline (as in the tar sands) on when a well must be reclaimed, and wells decommissioned before 1963 are exempt from today's provincial cleanup rules. Reclamation costs vary from $10,000 to over $1-million per well, with the total liability to reclaim all well sites, pipelines and other infrastructure now estimated at $19-billion, which is $4-billion more than the estimated accrued liability for oil sands mines.[78]

The most controversial of CAPP's ads shows Shelley Powell, an engineer and executive at Suncor Energy, using a spatula to swirl dark-grey tailings in a beaker. She says:

> Tailings results when we extract the bitumen from the oil sands. It's essentially like yogurt, and if left on its own would take decades to settle. The new technology that we've developed allows us to transform liquid materials in our tailings pond into this type of solid dry material in just a couple of weeks. This is a game changer. It's amazing to think that we can reclaim tailings ponds in a fraction of the amount of time that it had taken in the past.[79]

Ms. Powell seems to have forgotten that no tailings pond has actually ever been entirely reclaimed "in the past." Beyond that oversight, the ad uses several strategies to do two things: downplay the risks associated with tailings ponds and exaggerate the idea that technology will solve any problems quickly and easily. Perhaps the most egregious instance is the comparison of tailings to a dairy food like yogurt, which is definitely rubbish. While the consistency of tailings may be perceived to be similar to the consistency of yogurt, the rather more significant differences are enormous. Unlike yogurt, which many of us find tasty and nutritious, tailings contain arsenic, mercury and a host of other toxins that can cause cancer and other serious diseases. Because tailings ponds leak as much as 12 million litres of toxic liquid a day, it is possible (though not proven) that they are contributing to higher than normal cancer rates downstream of the bitumen mine. Further study is needed to confirm or disprove this; either way, leaving out the lethal nature of the contents of her beaker, and the inconvenient fact that tailings ponds leak millions of gallons of toxic soup into the underlying water table every day, is an egregious perversion of the facts.

Sierra Club Canada felt this ad was so grossly

misleading that it made a formal complaint to Advertising Standards Canada, a self-policing, industry-run advertising watchdog. The club alleged that CAPP had violated the "accuracy and clarity" clause of the Canadian Code of Advertising Standards, which stipulates in part that "advertisements must not contain inaccurate, deceptive or otherwise misleading claims ... [and] must not omit relevant information in a manner that, in the result, is deceptive." The Code adds that, in assessing an ad under this clause, "the concern is not with the intent of the sender or precise legality of the presentation. Rather, the focus is on the message ... as received or perceived, i.e., the general impression conveyed by the advertisement." The Sierra Club argued that the CAPP commercial failed to reflect the numerous environmental risks and health impacts of bitumen production.[80]

Janet Annesley, on the other hand, maintained that the yogurt–tailings comparison was simply meant to illuminate for the public the physical consistency of the tailings,[81] a claim Sierra Club executive director John Bennett dismissed out of hand. "The intent was not to talk about it being gooey. The intent clearly was to make the tar sands less toxic and less scary." He said this claim was borne out by all of the ads CAPP has broadcast about bitumen extraction, which are simply disarming first-person accounts that belie the true nature of what's really going on: "'I want to protect my environment and how we're doing this new, innovative thing that's making it all okay.' These things are designed to lessen the scary impact of the huge industrial development and toxic tailings."[82]

Advertising Standards Canada dismissed the Sierra Club's complaint. The decision, which was not unanimous, concluded that the comparison with the dairy product was fair because it "referred only to the apparent physical consistency of the tailings and did not humanize or soft-pedal the more controversial aspects surrounding tailings."[83] Wrote CAPP's Annesley: "We are pleased with ASC's finding that the oil and gas industry's ad is not misleading.... The tailings reclamation proof point will go back on air minus reference to yogurt, just to remove any potential misunderstanding."[84]

Royal Dutch Shell was not so lucky when it was taken to task for a similar transgression. When the World Wildlife Fund complained that the

Anglo-Dutch energy giant misled the public about the green credentials of its bitumen project in Alberta, the UK's Advertising Standards Authority agreed. Shell had published an advertisement alongside its financial results in a 2008 issue of the *Financial Times*, claiming: "We invest today's profits in tomorrow's solutions.... A growing world needs more energy, but at the same time we need to find new ways of managing carbon emissions to limit climate change. Continued investment in technology is one of the key ways we are able to address this challenge, and continue to secure a profitable and sustainable future."[85]

This is exactly the same kind of disingenuous messaging use by other oil companies, CAPP and even the Alberta government. The World Wildlife Fund did not agree with Shell's claims, of course, and complained that extracting and upgrading low-grade bitumen was not sustainable at all. Instead, WWF argued, the process is highly inefficient, destroys huge tracts of forest and emits millions of tons of GHGs. In its defence, Shell maintained that new technology was reducing pollution from its Athabasca oil sands project.

The Advertising Standards Authority must

have had its bullshit detector turned on, because it ruled in the WWF's favour. It concluded that Shell should not have used the word "sustainable" to describe its bitumen project and another scheme to build North America's biggest oil refinery. Both projects would lead to more GHG emissions, the ASA ruled, so the advertisement had breached rules on substantiation, truthfulness and environmental claims.[86]

"We considered that the Department for Environment, Food and Rural Affairs' (Defra's) best practice guidance on environmental claims stated that green claims should not be vague or ambiguous, for instance by simply trying to give a good impression about general concern for the environment," said the ASA in its ruling. "Defra had made that recommendation because, although 'sustainable' was a widely used term, the lack of a universally agreed definition meant that it was likely to be ambiguous and unclear to consumers. Because we had not seen data that showed how Shell was effectively managing carbon emissions from its oil sands projects in order to limit climate change, we concluded that the ad was misleading."[87]

Such disingenuous advertising campaigns are what University of British Columbia philosopher Alan Richardson calls "performative bullshit." Claims made by the Triple Alliance that they or their activities are or will become sustainable "has the form of a commitment, but it is not a real commitment." Corporations and governments know they have not made a commitment, but they act as if one were in effect in order to deflect public concern about future impacts. This happens all the time, not least in promises politicians make to get themselves elected, and it undermines the integrity of public discourse. Says Richardson, "Performative bullshit is the source of much of the sense many of us have that the world is making us crazy."[88]

"I think industry likes it that way," says David Schindler, whose scientific research has helped put the lie to many such claims:

> As long as there's confusion, there won't be
> any regulation. I've seen this with phosphates
> in detergents, with acid rain, with Big
> Tobacco. We're seeing it as we speak with
> climate. It's a standard industry tactic. Get

all sorts of voices so there's a muddle and it appears that the teeter-totter swings and it doesn't tip one way. And every year that you can get away with lack of regulation is a few billion more bucks in your pocket. After 40 years, I'm pretty sick of seeing this tactic fool people time after time. Maybe we all did just fall off a turnip truck.[89]

Why does the Triple Alliance use such deceitful tactics? Because they work. Too many of us seem to have either just fallen off that turnip truck or never got on it in the first place. Most of us just want to believe that things are not as bad as they are; we don't want to believe that our addiction to oil is not a problem, that the good, honest, hardworking people "just like us" that we see in the oil industry's advertising campaigns are more dependable than those nasty truth-hating environmentalists that make everything seem so bleak.

Just ask Tzeporah Berman. Berman is a mother of two and co-director of Greenpeace International's Climate and Energy Program. Her recent book *This Crazy Time*, chronicling her activism over the past two decades, inspired Bill

McKibben to dub her "a modern environmental hero." *Reader's Digest* called her "Canada's Queen of Green." She was one of six Canadian nominees for the Schwab Social Entrepreneur of the Year Award, and UTNE *Reader* profiled her as one of "50 Visionaries Changing the World." She is as fierce an opponent of the tar sands as there is.

You can imagine Berman's surprise when she arrived home from a weeks-long business trip to Europe to meet with climate and energy campaigners from around the world to find her 8-year-old son extolling the virtues of the tar sands. The Berman family had just sat down for supper at one of their favourite Chinese restaurants when he blurted, as only a child who had just learned some electrifying new fact about the world could blurt, that all was well in tarsandsland. "Mommy, isn't it great that they have figured out how to do the oil sands better?!" he said excitedly. "Now we can get oil that we really need while leaving the forests, and even the butterflies are okay."

"What?!" Berman sputtered, showering her husband in green tea. "What. Are. You. Talking. About?"

Quinn explained that he had seen commercials

on the television. "A lot." There, along with Dora and Barney, he had met the "nice people who had fixed all the problems" his mother was campaigning so vigorously to redress. Innocent and hopeful, he was relieved to know that "all the nature is fine, because after they get the oil we need, they pat dirt back on and plant flowers and trees."[90]

Quinn Berman's revelation occurred during the same week of October 2011 that the federal environment commissioner released a report that concluded the Harper government had no plan to achieve even its own pathetic climate change targets, and that "decisions about oil sands projects have been based on incomplete, poor or non-existent environmental information that has, in turn, led to poorly informed decisions."[91] But, for some reason, those inconvenient conclusions did not make it into the oil industry's advertising campaign. Go figure.

Breaking All the Rules

Once upon a time people did grievous harm to the environment without fully understanding the consequences of their actions. That defence is no longer available, and that sure knowledge we now have entails equally sure moral obligations.

—JONATHON PORRITT, former chair, Sustainable Development Commission

In January 2012, at the Calgary Chamber of Commerce, after assuring the uneasy audience that he wasn't one of the "environmental radicals" on the government's watch list, federal Minister of the Environment Peter Kent boasted that Canada was a "world-class regulator" with an "absolutely firm and unwavering " commitment to protecting Canada's natural heritage.[92] Two months later, Alberta Premier Alison Redford reinforced Kent's claims, in a speech to the US Energy Association.

"It's important to rise above rhetoric and emotions and get the facts out," she said. "Alberta is home to some of the strictest environmental regulations in the world." After all, she emphasized, Alberta was the first North American government to impose greenhouse gas emission limits.[93]

Redford and Kent's upbeat characterization of Canada's environmental performance is often used to justify claims that the Alberta and Canadian governments are developing the tar sands in a clean, responsible, sustainable, even ethical manner. Tar sands supporters might think it churlish to quibble about such claims, but let's do it anyway, for the truth is rather less sanguine than Canada's politicians would have us believe.

It surprises almost everyone I talk to that Canada has some of the weakest environmental legislation in the developed world. Dr. David R. Boyd, an environmental lawyer and author of *Unnatural Law: Rethinking Canadian Environmental Law and Policy*, wrote recently that it is "an incontrovertible fact" that Canada is an international laggard in environmental policy and practice.[94] Unlike Kent and Redford, Boyd points to a litany of reputable sources to support his claim. For instance, in 2009 the Conference Board of Canada, the foremost independent, not-for-profit, applied-research organization in the country, ranked Canada 15th out of 17 wealthy industrialized nations on environmental performance. A year later, researchers at Simon Fraser University ranked Canada 24th out of 25 OECD nations on environmental performance. Researchers at Yale and Columbia universities, in their 2012 Environmental Performance Index, ranked Canada 37th, far behind green leaders like Sweden, Norway and Costa Rica, and trailing major industrial economies including Germany, France, Japan and Brazil. They also concluded that Canada's performance is deteriorating, ranking just 52nd in terms of progress between 2000 and 2010. Even Prime Minister Harper has candidly admitted that "Canada's environmental performance is, by most measures, the worst in the developed world. We've got big problems."[95]

Anthony Perl and Eugene Lee, academic experts in Canadian environmental policy and the editors of *The Integrity Gap*, an aptly named book on Canada's environmental policy, identified several reasons for Canada's poor performance in the realm of environmental management. The most obvious is the disproportionate political influence of the natural resources industry, including Big Oil, which tends to oppose bearing either the costs or the constraints associated with environmental protection. There's also the small matter of bureaucratic insensitivity and indifference, which prevents government officials from taking a leadership role in environmental protection. Finally, it seems that Canada's political institutions are simply not up to the task of resolving the controversies generated by contemporary environmental challenges in a country that relies so heavily on clear-cutting trees, mining coal and pumping oil for its economic well-being.

Part of the problem is that environmental roles and responsibilities in Canada are about as clear as a tar sands tailings pond. Under Canada's Constitution, the federal and provincial governments share responsibility for protecting the environment. Provinces have primary jurisdiction over natural resource sectors such as forestry, water, mining and hydroelectric development. The federal government is responsible for fisheries, fish habitat, navigation and shipping, Aboriginal lands and treaties, interprovincial issues and criminal law. It also has residual powers related to areas not specifically assigned to the provinces.[96] This ensures that provincial and federal governments are in almost constant conflict over how, even whether, to use environmental laws and regulations to protect Canada's air, water, forests and wildlife habitats from environmental degradation.

Nowhere are these problems more apparent than in the realm of environmental assessment (EA), which has been a major factor in the Triple Alliance's claims of "responsible, clean and sustainable" tar sands development. EA procedures allow regulators to identify and assess the environmental, social and economic consequences of proposed industrial projects. Major tar sands projects trigger EAs both federally under the Canadian Environmental Assessment Act (CEAA) and at the provincial level through Alberta's Energy Resources Conservation Board. Because the federal and Alberta governments amended and signed the Canada–Alberta Agreement on Environmental Assessment Cooperation in 2005, environmental assessment of major industrial projects, such as tar sands extraction, may be a combined effort, called a joint review panel, which must consider the project's incremental impact on cumulative or combined effects. Ostensibly this process assists bureaucrats in determining whether such projects should be approved, and if so, under what conditions. The goal is to prevent harmful projects from being built and to ensure that those that are approved are better planned and less environmentally and socially risky or harmful than perhaps they might otherwise have been.

In 2003 William Leiss, a scientist at the University of Ottawa and one of Canada's foremost experts in environmental assessment and risk management, wrote in *The Integrity Gap* that "Canada has an embarrassing and consistent record of failure in credible environmental assessment for high-profile, large development projects...."[97] The Royal Society of Canada, in its 2010 review of the environmental and health impacts of the tar sands, found that the environmental regulatory capacity of the Alberta and federal governments was lacking, and characterized the environmental impact assessment process used by regulators to make public interest decisions as "seriously deficient" and falling short of international standards.[98]

The preamble to the 1992 Canadian Environmental Assessment Act stated that "environmental assessment provides an effective means of integrating environmental factors into planning and decision-making processes in a manner that promotes sustainable development." [NB: while this book was in production, the 1992 Act was repealed and replaced by a 2012 CEAA which does not have a preamble; please see the second and third parts of note 98.] One of the purposes of the 1992 Act, as expressed in s. 4(1)(a), was "to ensure that projects are considered in a careful and precautionary manner before federal authorities take action in connection with them, in order to ensure that such projects do not cause significant adverse environmental effects." [See now s. 4(1)(a), (b) of the 2012 Act.]

The federal environmental assessment process begins when a federal authority becomes involved, whether as project proponent, regulator, land manager or funding source. Before exercising its powers in relation to a project, the responsible authority must ensure that the EA is performed and that it takes into account the significance of all harmful or undesirable effects on the environment that are expected to remain after proposed mitigation measures are put into place.

Since 2000, four of Alberta's tar sands mines – Canadian Natural Resources' Horizon project, Shell's Jackpine and Muskeg River mines and Imperial Oil's Kearl project – have undergone joint reviews. A fifth undertaking, Suncor's Project Millennium, had undergone a comprehensive review in 1999. In October 2011 Canada's commissioner of the environment and sustainable development released another damning report. Scott Vaughan examined whether the federal government considered cumulative environmental effects of major tar sands projects in northern Alberta in accordance with the environmental assessment process established by the Canadian Environmental Assessment Act. The findings were sobering.

According to commissioner Vaughan's report, submissions prepared by federal authorities for these five environmental assessments "repeatedly pointed to gaps in environmental data and scientific information related to the potential cumulative impact of oil sands projects on water quantity and quality, fish and fish habitat, land and wildlife, and air." The submissions also pointed to "insufficient information on the potential acidification of water bodies in northern Saskatchewan; a lack of baseline data for assessing the impact of projects on wildlife corridors; and uncertainties and incomplete information regarding the impacts of stream flow rates, tailings, and other water issues, such as the potential impact of polycyclic aromatic hydrocarbons extending as far as Great Slave Lake."[99]

"In 2004," the report continued, "Environment Canada noted that the rate of oil sands project development was potentially exceeding the ability of the Cumulative Environmental Management Association (CEMA) and the Regional Sustainable Development Strategy to introduce effective management systems to set environmental thresholds or objectives. Similarly, the joint review panel for the 2007 Kearl Oil Sands Project stated that while the success of CEMA is critical, ultimately, government regulators are responsible for managing environmental effects in the region."[100]

Every so often, someone contests a joint review panel's approval of a tar sands project. Several environmental organizations, including the

Alberta-based Pembina Institute, challenged the joint panel's conclusion that the Kearl tar sands project would not likely result in significant adverse environmental effects, at least once proposed mitigation measures were taken into account. In particular, the Pembina was concerned that cumulative effects management, climate-altering greenhouse gas emissions and impacts on water and endangered species, particularly woodland caribou, had not been adequately assessed. And so the Pembina went before Madam Justice Tremblay-Lamer in Federal Court in what would come to be known as "the Kearl Mines case."

The decision, perhaps not surprisingly, went the industry's way. With respect to cumulative effects management, water and endangered species, the court chose to defer to the joint panel's assessment of the evidence provided in Kearl's environmental assessment, which was that either the cumulative impacts were not significant or they could be mitigated. Justice Tremblay-Lamer held that the Pembina was simply challenging the quality or thoroughness of the evidence that had been before the joint panel, and without actually vetting that evidence, she decided that the panel was the expert.[101] Quoting from a 1996 decision by the Federal Court of Appeal, Justice Tremblay-Lamer concurred that "'[r]easonable people can and do disagree about the adequacy and completeness of evidence which forecasts future results and about the significance of such results without thereby raising questions of law.'" The judge did not consider whether the evidence in the Kearl environmental assessment was accurate or persuasive; she simply concluded that it was not her place to judge.[102]

In doing so, the court implicitly accepted Imperial's claim that peatlands (a type of wetland), which are destroyed by tar sands mining, could be reclaimed, even though Imperial agreed with the Pembina that just how peatlands were to be reclaimed "is not even known in general terms."[103] This is also the conclusion reached in one of Alberta Environment's own reports; and David Schindler confirmed in a peer-reviewed paper that "reclamation of peatlands has so far proven impossible."[104] Indeed, Alberta Environment's 2007 *Provincial Wetland Restoration/Compensation Guide* concluded that "it is almost impossible to fully replicate the complexity of a natural wetland ecosystem."[105] No matter. Imperial simply argued that the "dynamic nature of follow-up measures and adaptive management will resolve initial uncertainties," and Madam Justice Tremblay-Lamer agreed.

Likewise, Imperial Oil argued that, some 60 years hence, it could simply cover Kearl's massive toxic tailings ponds with several metres of freshwater and create, in several years, what industry euphemistically calls "end pit lakes" (EPLs) that could support fish.[106] This is inconsistent with CEMA's conclusion that "the development of EPLs as a natural reclamation tool for process-affected waters raises issues of concern for regulators and stakeholders. Much of this concern results from the fact that historical data are insufficient to determine a realistic outcome of the final features of EPLs. Modelling and relevant background studies have been the basis of research, but a fully realized EPL has yet to be constructed."[107] The joint environmental assessment panel itself had concluded that the transformation of tailings ponds into healthy end-pit lakes was dependent on the development of future science and technology, and while Justice Tremblay-Lamer acknowledged there was some uncertainty with respect to end pit lake technology, "the existing level of uncertainty is not such that it should paralyze the entire project."[108] The precautionary principle, which the Canadian Environmental Assessment Act requires to be exercised in all circumstances, was ignored in favour of a cornucopian belief in science and technology to solve, at some uncertain time in the future, any and all problems.

The issue over greenhouse gas emissions related to the project was rather more complicated and resulted in a partial, though ultimately meaningless, victory for the Pembina and the rest of the environmental community. The court ruled that the assessment panel had erred in law by failing to provide a rationale to support its conclusion that the adverse environmental effects of increased greenhouse gas emissions would be either insignificant or mitigated. Wrote Justice Tremblay-Lamer: "The panel dismissed as insignificant the greenhouse gas emissions without any rationale as to why the intensity-based mitigation would be effective to reduce the greenhouse gas emissions, equivalent to 800,000 passenger vehicles, to a level of insignificance. Without this vital link – the clear and cogent articulation of the reasons behind the panel's conclusion – the deference accorded to its expertise is not triggered."[109] Accordingly, the judge ordered the panel to provide a rationale for its conclusion. It did and Imperial's Kearl tar sands mine was approved.

Perhaps the most discouraging part of the environmental assessment process is that, despite the innumerable warnings and challenges and failures over the last decade, little has changed in the way environmental assessments are conducted. The terms of reference issued to proponents of tar sands projects are always "generic and d[o] not change from one project assessment to the next."[110] For the five projects reviewed by commissioner Vaughan, the "federal government did not take the opportunity to modify terms of reference in later projects to deal with key concerns previously raised by federal authorities, in areas such as water quantity and quality, fish and fish habitat, land and wildlife, and air. In our opinion, federal authorities should have used the sound management practice of adapting terms of reference over time in order to address identified gaps in information being provided to them."[111]

When I asked William Leiss, who had so roundly criticized Canada's environmental assessment process in 2003, if things had improved over the last nine years, he had this to say: "Things are probably worse now, since the federal EA process is being systematically dismantled, environmental review increasingly politicized, and climate change action is dead in the water, and will remain so. What's to celebrate? As far as the oil sands is concerned, I regard the December 2010 [Royal Society] expert panel report to be the definitive story, and it does not inspire confidence."[112]

The EA process in Canada is, in essence, a mummer's farce that provides the illusion of "clean, responsible and sustainable" development without actually having to achieve it. Meanwhile, the Alberta and federal governments continue to assess and approve tar sands projects based on RAMP's condemned monitoring results. In early December 2011, federal Natural Resources Minister Joe Oliver approved the tar sands' sixth open-pit mine, Total's 100,000-barrel-a-day Joslyn South project. Eleven more mines have been approved and are (or soon will be) under construction. Three weeks after Oliver's announcement, the Alberta Energy Resources

Conservation Board and Alberta Environment & Water approved Athabasca Oil Sands' 150,000-barrel-per-day MacKay River project, one of 33 in situ projects that have recently been given the go-ahead. Three more mines and 17 additional in situ projects are currently being reviewed – all based on RAMP's faulty monitoring. By the time the new monitoring program has provided any meaningful data, tar sands production will have doubled to more than 3.5 million barrels per day.

Despite these rather sobering condemnations of the nature and application of Canada's legislative and regulatory framework, the federal government, led by ultra-conservative Prime Minister Stephen Harper, is in the process of weakening the EA process even further. Proposed changes to the Fisheries Act and the EA process put forward in 2012 by the Harper government will more expediently approve tar sands projects, not to mention the proposed Northern Gateway pipeline, which would transport bitumen crude across central British Columbia to ports on the West Coast, where it would then be transported through perilous ocean waters in large tankers on its way to Asia (specifically China).

The Fisheries Act, one of Canada's strongest pieces of environmental legislation and a real bother to most industrial projects – including those in the tar sands – is being gutted. The current Act makes it illegal to damage fish habitat, but the proposed changes replace any reference to "habitat" with vague wording that will be even more difficult to enforce. Given that the Royal Society's expert panel concluded that Canada is already failing to meet its national and international commitments to sustain and protect marine biodiversity, it's not surprising that two former Conservative fisheries ministers and more than 600 scientists – including 18 fellows of the Royal Society and more than 30 endowed research chairs – have opposed the changes. But Keith Ashfield, Harper's stalwart fisheries minister, is steadfast in his belief that Canada's current, protective policies "do not reflect the priorities of Canadians"[113] – despite poll after poll showing that Canadians do prioritize environmental protection over economic development.

The CEAA process too is being gutted. Harper's Conservative government is slashing the Canadian Environmental Assessment Agency's budget by 40 per cent and imposing arbitrary new timelines for regulatory review of major industrial projects.[114] Natural Resources Minister Joe Oliver has said that the changes will be retroactively applied to reviews on projects that are already underway, such as the contentious Northern Gateway pipeline.[115] When I asked Richard Lindgren, senior counsel for the Canadian Environmental Law Association, what he thought of the proposed amendments, he said, "They would collectively set back federal [environmental assessment] law by at least 40 years. The recommendations are primarily aimed at speeding up approvals for mega-projects, rather than implementing the actual reforms necessary to ensure that CEAA does the job envisioned by Parliament."[116]

But oil is a global commodity, and its continued use in the age of climate change is also threatened by environmental legislation and regulation in other countries. Rather than pass laws and regulations at home to reduce carbon emissions from tar sands production, the governments of Canada and Alberta have been working hand in hand with the oil industry to undermine progressive efforts to reduce carbon emissions all over the world.

In the United States, the Triple Alliance has successfully lobbied to undermine several bills that include low-carbon fuel standards that would make it difficult or impossible to use tar sands crude as a feedstock for transportation fuels. In 2005, under the watchful eye of the Alberta Minister of International & Intergovernmental Affairs at the time, Gary Mar, the provincial government opened its own office in the Canadian Embassy on Washington, DC's Pennsylvania Avenue and began working with the oil-industry-funded American Petroleum Institute to discourage state governments from adopting low-carbon fuel standards.[117] Premier Ed Stelmach applauded Mar for convincing legislators to drop Maryland's Oil Sands Responsibility Act, which would have prohibited state agencies from purchasing high-carbon fuel derived from Alberta's bitumen. Mar's convincing advocacy also encouraged Wisconsin policymakers to drop their proposed low-carbon fuel standard,[118] and he claims to have helped put the kibosh on similar bills in Minnesota and Michigan too.[119]

How did Gary Mar do it? According to environmental advocates working the halls in

DC, Mar downplayed the industry's ecological impacts and accentuated the economic and energy security benefits. The back side of Mar's business card, for instance, read: "Did you know Alberta ... oil sands produce only one tenth of one per cent of the world's greenhouse gases."[120] Like the oil industry, Mar downplayed the environmental impacts, framing them as tiny, surmountable challenges that can be addressed with as yet untested or undeveloped technology. Danielle Droitsch, an American environmental lawyer who has worked in both Alberta and Washington, says that the Canadian and Alberta governments' sales pitch is effective because many American policymakers take it at face value for the truth. "The message in Washington has been that there are no problems with the oil sands industry at all," she says. "If a US decision maker who's very busy and has lots of things on their mind is being approached constantly by the Canadian embassy and government of Alberta, then that decision maker doesn't have balanced information."[121]

Gary Doer, Canada's current ambassador to the United States and a man once recognized by *Business Week* magazine as one of the world's most committed climate change champions, is now considered one of the top bitumen lobbyists in Washington, DC. As soon as he arrived in the nation's capital in October 2009, Doer told the *Financial Post* that the tar sands was getting an unfair amount of criticism about its impact on the climate.[122] Since then, Doer has spent much of his time and energy promoting Canada's booming bitumen industry and fighting against US laws to reduce climate-change-causing greenhouse gases, all part of the Department of Foreign Affairs "oil sands advocacy strategy."[123] On November 3, 2011, he even sent a formal letter to Lisa Jackson, head of the US Environmental Protection Agency, to lobby on behalf of TransCanada's application to build the controversial Keystone XL pipeline, which would ferry bitumen crude to the Gulf Coast for upgrading and export. "We are concerned with the EPA's recommendation that extraction-related GHG emissions in Canada form part of the Environmental Impact Statement included in the permitting process," he wrote, adding that both nations have historically adopted environmental assessment regimes that "complement" each other, "while respecting the sovereignty of our independent decision-making processes." Jackson was not intimidated. "Given that the possible consequences of greenhouse-gas emissions are global in nature," she replied in a letter of her own, "they include potential impacts on the United States, and we believe that it is appropriate that the State Department consider these upstream greenhouse-gas emissions in its evaluation."[124]

"Numerous employees in the Canadian Embassy's Washington Advocacy Secretariat, which includes the Province of Alberta's office, are engaged in various aspects of energy advocacy, as is the Ambassador and other sections within the Embassy," a spokesperson told *Embassy* magazine. "Given the importance of the Canada–us energy relationship, energy advocacy also extends well beyond the Embassy to regional and local levels through our network of 22 offices across the us."[125]

A similar strategy is being used in Europe, where the European Union is attempting to reduce greenhouse gas emissions by implementing a low-carbon fuel standard. Unlike most governments, including Canada's, the EU is actually trying to reduce emissions of greenhouse gases. The EU's Fuel Quality Directive is part of the effort to reduce carbon emissions from the transportation sector by 20 per cent by 2030. The directive discourages the use of relatively dirty sources of transport fuel by categorizing various types of fuel according to their carbon intensity and penalizing the most polluting.

In September 2009 Kevin Stringer, a senior official at Natural Resources Canada, pointed out in a letter that "many European-based oil companies such as British Petroleum, Royal Dutch Shell, Statoil and Total" are active players in Canada's tar sands.[126] Ross Hornby, Canada's ambassador to the EU, followed up with a tersely worded letter to the Director General of the EU's Environment Directorate in January 2010, arguing that the fuel quality proposal would create "a large administrative burden and prohibitive costs." Incredibly, he also claimed that the attempt to differentiate bitumen from other types of fuels is "not science-based," and constitutes "unjustifiable discrimination against the oil sands." [127] Canada has even threatened to lodge a complaint with the World Trade Organization if the EU passes the Fuel Quality Directive.

Alas, an analysis by Stanford University's

Adam Brandt indicates that Hornby was just blowing smoke. Tar sands crude is not, in fact, the dirtiest source of oil identified in the regulations. While conventional oil is assigned a default GHG intensity value of 87.1 grams of carbon dioxide per megajoule of energy (gCO_2/MJ), turning coal into liquid fuel is almost twice that amount (172 gCO_2/MJ). Tar sands oil sits somewhere in the middle, at 107.3 gCO_2/MJ. And any tar sands producer that can demonstrate that its oil is less than the default value is welcome to do so, which would put it in a better market position relative to other, dirtier sources. It is, in other words, a system that encourages better performance from tar sands producers, something that is sorely needed as GHG emissions from Alberta's tar sands continue to skyrocket.

Although the decision should have been made more than a year ago, the EU has yet to implement or scrap the Fuel Quality Directive, in part because Canada's almost daily lobbying of European officials has been successful at swaying some member states. The EU's initial attempt to pass the directive in February 2012 ended in deadlock. EU officials needed a three-quarters majority to approve the measure, which would have led to the proposal passing quickly into law. At the vote, there were 89 in favour of the proposal, 128 against and 128 abstentions. The impasse meant that the decision was referred to EU ministers, who have decided to conduct a full impact assessment on the new proposal before submitting a proposal in 2013.

"With all the lobbying against the proposal, I feared member states would reject the proposal," said Connie Hedegaard, the EU commissioner for climate action. "I am glad that this was not the case. I hope ministers will realise that unconventional fuels need to account for their considerably higher emissions through separate values."[128]

Why are Canada's attempts to encourage foreign governments to abandon progressive energy policy so egregious? First, the argument relies almost solely on the selective use of scientific information to make claims that are not all that connected to or concerned with the truth. Second, even conservative think tanks like the C.D. Howe Institute recognize that in a climate-changing world, we need progressive legislation and policy that puts carbon-intensive fuels at a competitive disadvantage to reduce greenhouse gas emissions and encourages the development of alternative, low-carbon energy sources. If Alberta's bitumen is going to be the clean, responsible and sustainable source of energy that government officials and industry spokespeople tout it as, the industry is going to have to manufacture it in a way that greatly reduces the GHG emissions and other environmental impacts. To date, there has been no real progress on solving that problem, and in fact GHG emissions per barrel of bitumen crude have been increasing.

If the Triple Alliance is serious about its commitment to reducing GHG emissions from tar sands oil, the pace and scope of development will need to be slowed until the requisite technologies are in place. But instead, the Triple Alliance's strategy has been to simply reframe the debate in terms more favourable to the status quo. Rather than simply ignoring or understating the environmental risks and challenges, they have begun to prey on our deepest fears to promote bitumen development as the solution to America's energy security and the future of our collective economic health. The former, of course, is something Mark Evans would immediately identify as rubbish or irretrievable speculation. CAPP and the Government of Alberta like to claim that a safe, secure source of oil from a friendly nation can further enhance US security by reducing imports from less secure and reliable sources like Venezuela, Nigeria and the Middle East. The argument also suggests that this would reduce the amount of revenue in the pockets of unfriendly authoritarian regimes that support terrorism and eschew democracy. These claims appear to have little connection to the truth. The United States has consumed approximately 19 million barrels of oil per day for the last decade, 63 per cent of which is imported from foreign countries. Canada is the United States' biggest single-country supplier, providing approximately 20 per cent of America's imported oil. Even the most optimistic predictions suggest that Canada's bitumen bonanza can supply only about one-third of America's addiction in the coming decades – and it will be the most expensive oil on the planet.

Even if America's internal supplies experience some resurgence, the US will still be reliant on oil from countries it does not want to support. However much oil Canada produces and exports to the US, its production will not reduce revenues to the despots in other, less friendly nations.

Research by the Council on Foreign Relations, an independent, non-partisan US think tank Prime Minister Harper called the most respected and influential organization on foreign policy, found that "because oil is essentially traded on a global market, [the security benefits of Canada's bitumen are] not as large as some might intuitively assume. Oilsands exploitation will not fundamentally change the global oil picture."[129]

The most significant problem with the Triple Alliance's claims is that in the age of climate change, there is no longer an "environmentally sound" way to develop and use hydrocarbons – including Alberta's tar sands – for energy production. But this hasn't stopped them as such anyway. When Canadian climate modeller Andrew Weaver and one of his graduate students, Neil Swart, published their research in *Nature Climate Change* in February 2012,[130] they concluded that developing and burning every last drop of the tar sands would warm the planet by about 0.36°C, equivalent to about half the warming that's been observed so far. But not all of the tar sands is recoverable with current technology; when Weaver and Swart considered only the tar sands proven to be economically viable, that number dropped to 0.03°C. The real culprits, they concluded, were the much larger global reserves of natural gas and coal, which would result in 3°C and 15°C warming respectively.

The Triple Alliance welcomed Weaver and Swart's findings with the same certainty Pope Urban VIII must have felt as he watched the sun rise in the east and set in the west, "proving" beyond a reasonable doubt that the sun revolved around Earth. Canada's bombastic Natural Resources Minister Joe Oliver told the *Globe and Mail* that he hoped "this will put to rest some of the wild exaggerations and misstatements from too many people who ought to know better," adding that he planned to incorporate the report's numbers into future speeches.[131] Likewise, CAPP took the opportunity to applaud the results, hoping they would help calm "the inflamed rhetoric from the other side."[132]

Dr. Weaver, who is one of Canada's most respected climate scientists and a lead author on many of the United Nations Intergovernmental Panel on Climate Change's reports, responded with surprise at the reception of his analysis. In a public statement, he said, "It would be a huge mistake to interpret our results as some kind of a 'get out of jail free' card for the tar sands. While coal is the greatest threat to the climate globally, the tar sands remain the largest source of greenhouse gas emission growth in Canada and are the single largest reason Canada is failing to meet its international climate commitments and failing to be a climate leader. The world needs to transition away from fossil fuels. That means coal, unconventional gas, and unconventional oil all need to addressed."[133]

Mark Jaccard, a professor at Simon Fraser University and an expert in energy-economy modelling, took Weaver's response one step further. In an op-ed in the *Globe and Mail*, Jaccard tried to stem the tide of pro-tar-sands rhetoric that Weaver and Swart's research had unleashed. He explained that it is already too late to prevent a 2°C increase in average global temperatures because of the amount of GHGs already in the atmosphere and the inertia in our global energy system. Pointing to a report from MIT's Joint Program on the Science and Policy of Global Change, Jaccard maintained that our only hope of keeping climate change below 4°C is to immediately reduce emissions in all sectors of the economy, starting with rich countries. "We can't allow any expansion of the tar sands," he wrote, and the Keystone XL and Northern Gateway pipelines that would support expanded fossil fuel use should not be built. "The [MIT] report shows how and why the Canadian tar sands must contract immediately as part of a global effort to prevent a four-degree increase in temperature and catastrophic climate change."[134]

The Triple Alliance simply cannot acknowledge that the age of hydrocarbons is over. This seems logical, of course, given that their economic self-interest is so inextricably tied to the status quo, but it is also a dangerous form of narcissistic delusion. It is too late for Alberta's bitumen to make Canada an energy superpower or enhance American energy security. It will only make a few corporations and their shareholders enormously rich, in large part by externalizing the social and environmental costs they will impose on the rest of us. Although it is true that bitumen production accounts for only 1 per cent of global GHG emissions, the risks associated with the commodity it produces and the precedent it sets – that any and all oil deposits, no matter where they are found or how dirty or risky they are to produce – are just too high.

If we proceed as the Triple Alliance suggests, and fossil-energy consumption continues without any changes in government policy, the International Energy Agency concludes it "takes us inexorably towards a long-term concentration of greenhouse gases in the atmosphere in excess of 1,000 parts per million of carbon dioxide equivalent." This would result in the global average temperature rising by up to 6°C, which "would lead almost certainly to massive climatic change and irreparable damage to the planet."[135] This is the legacy that the Triple Alliance's vision of the future would leave for our children and generations to come, and it would leave them with a debt they will never be able to repay.

Rethinking Advocacy

People who shut their eyes to reality simply invite their own destruction, and anyone who insists on remaining in a state of innocence long after that innocence is dead turns himself into a monster.
—JAMES BALDWIN, *Notes of a Native Son*

The escalation of the Triple Alliance's little black lies were too much for Michael Marx. From his perspective, the environmental community, believing the facts were on their side, were trying to win the Great Bitumen War by providing the public with more data on the risks and dangers the Triple Alliance was either ignoring or hiding. This strategy, he felt, was necessary but not sufficient to turn the tide of public opinion. Polling indicated that Canadians – a decidedly conservative, risk-averse and often apathetic bunch – were concerned about the social and environmental impacts of the tar sands, but they also seemed to believe that the resource was being, or at least could be, developed in the "clean, sustainable and responsible" way government and industry claimed. Although a vociferous minority of concerned citizens continued to raise the alarm, the *vox populi* was rather silent on the issue. Marx thought the environmental community had to do something different; they had to find a way to raise the stakes.

Marx is not your average environmentalist. Like many of the PR professionals and lobbyists who work for Big Oil and the governments that court it, he is a professional persuader. In fact, he used to work for big business. Marx received his doctorate from the University of Wisconsin–Madison, where he studied social psychology, organizational behaviour, marketing and communications. "If there's one word to describe my PhD," he told me in a telephone interview from his San Francisco office, "it's persuasion."[136] Properly educated in the ways and means of manipulation, he went on to become the president of Selection Sciences Inc., a San Francisco–based management consulting firm, for 10 years. His clients included Hewlett-Packard, Memorex, Fireman's Fund,

Transamerica, Pacific Bell, American Express, Riggs Bank and other Fortune 1000 companies.

But Marx was not always all business; he spent some of his time and energy volunteering in the not-for-profit sector. While on the board of the Rainforest Action Network, he designed and directed the organization's international Boycott Mitsubishi campaign before turning his sights toward the successful campaign to protect British Columbia's Great Bear Rainforest. He eventually left his full-time business job to lead Corporate Ethics International, where he oversaw the design and implementation of a well-funded international tar sands campaign. This was a gargantuan task that involved working with almost 100 organizations in the US, Canada and Europe to stop the expansion of the tar sands, what Marx routinely calls "the most environmentally destructive energy project on earth."[137]

For most of the last two decades, most of the environmental community has adopted a rationalistic approach to its work. Although environmentalists make mistakes and occasionally follow their opponents into the murky waters of sophistry, almost all of them believe, with the conviction of religious fundamentalists, that educating the public with facts is their sole purpose in life. Combined with encouraging grassroots public support for protecting nature from the stressors humans impose on it, most environmentalists believe people armed with accurate information will do the right thing. They assume that if we can identify the problems and their science-based solutions, and put a little political pressure on decision makers, then those political leaders would surely follow suit and implement the solutions.

The Pembina Institute is perhaps the best example of this philosophy in action. An Alberta-based environmental think tank spawned by the Lodgepole sour-gas blowout in 1982 that left two people dead, Pembina was the first to raise the alarm about the devastating consequences of the rapid and unregulated development of Alberta's bitumen deposits. Pembina is also the only environmental group that chooses to use the term "oil sands" rather than "tar sands." The *Globe and Mail*, Canada's largest national newspaper, commented, "Pembina's strong research has won respect from the business community, and it even conducts consulting work for companies that want guidance to make their operations more sustainable." "[We] give them the frank, no-bullshit assessment," says Pembina executive director Ed Whittingham, "unlike a for-profit management consultancy that's going to tell them what they want to hear."[138]

At the same time, Pembina uses the facts to try and hold industry and government accountable in the public arena when they don't behave in ways the organization would call "responsible." Pembina has framed the bitumen issue as a failure of both the federal and provincial governments to adequately manage and regulate bitumen development. While acknowledging that industry has made significant improvements over the years, Pembina maintains that industry can and must do a better job of mitigating its impacts on the land, rivers and people of the tar sands region and beyond.

"I think there's a real opportunity to responsibly develop the oil sands," says the optimistic Whittingham, who was installed as Pembina's new executive director after completing his MBA and running the consulting side of Pembina's operations for several years. "... to develop it in a way that doesn't impair key environmental thresholds – for example, the Athabasca River, critical air sheds and critical habitat." Speaking with Peter McKenzie-Brown, a writer, historian and career oil industry public relations man who calls the Pembina "a unique Alberta success story," Whittingham added that he believes a collaborative, business-friendly model "is doable. I meet with industry people a lot and I find that many of them think it's doable, too."[139]

Although the Pembina was dismissed as a bastion of radical extremists by former Alberta Premier Ralph Klein and others, it's clear that Whittingham and his staff at the Pembina are one of the most respected environmental organizations working on the tar sands issue, in large part because they are very much concerned about and connected to the truth about Alberta's bitumen experiment. But it's hard to make the case that the rational approach alone was making much of a difference. Bitumen development in Alberta has exploded since the Pembina started making waves back in 1986, and there was little evidence that either the provincial or the federal government is interested in making good on their promises of clean, responsible and sustainable energy development.

In 2009 Michael Marx decided it was time to rethink Alberta. "I felt the Canadian groups were way too timid," says Marx. "They believe that facts and [policy] processes will lead to a reasonable outcome. My background and experience indicate this is not the case, especially when you're up against Big Oil. Rationality is not going to get us anywhere, and our funders are not in this in perpetuity."[140]

A growing body of research indicates that Marx is on to something. At some unconscious level, we are all bullshitters, unwittingly deceiving ourselves about the most important issues of our times. Few of us take humility seriously, and too many of us are overconfident in our ability to make accurate and objective judgments about the nature of reality around us. Optimism bias too can leave us susceptible to overestimating the likelihood of positive events (such as conservative governments' ability to manage Canada's bitumen production in a "responsible" and "sustainable" manner) and underestimating or ignoring the likelihood of negative events (such as the oil industry's propensity to leave great big messes in its wake).

Most of us are likely to make decisions based on our preconceived beliefs about the world – our *weltanschauung* – rather than a careful consideration of the facts. Otherwise intelligent people can deceive themselves to a point where "the facts" have no bearing on the choices they make or even the range of possible options before them. "The motivation to be accurate enhances use of those beliefs and strategies that are considered most appropriate, whereas the motivation to arrive at particular conclusions enhances use of those that are considered most likely to yield the desired conclusion," wrote the late Princeton psychologist Ziva Kunda in her award-winning paper on what she called "motivated reasoning." "There is considerable evidence that people are more likely to arrive at conclusions that they want to arrive at."[141]

Belief about the existence of anthropogenic climate change is an excellent example of the dangers of self-delusion. Despite almost unanimous acceptance of this scientific fact, and increasing evidence of the perilous consequences of our inaction, we still hear comments like this: "It's a hoax," said Don Blankenship, CEO of Massey Energy, in a 2010 debate on West Virginia public radio about climate change. Massey Energy is the sixth-largest coal company in the United States, and Blankenship likes to equate energy conservation and government regulation of industry with some inevitable slide toward communism.[142] "Clearly anyone that says they know what the temperature of the Earth is going to be in 2020 or 2030," he said, "needs to be put in an asylum because they don't."[143]

Such crazy talk is not surprising. Research by the Cultural Cognition Project, a group of scholars who study how cultural values shape public perceptions and policy beliefs, indicates that "people tend to conform their factual beliefs to ones that are consistent with their cultural outlook, their world view."[144] "Individualists" embrace authority, free enterprise and the cornucopian belief in new technology as the source of our wealth and the answer to our problems. "Communitarians," on the other hand, are suspicious of authority, commerce and industry.

Left or right, conservative or liberal, "the reason that people react in a closed-minded way to information is that the implications of it threaten their values," says Yale University law professor

Dan Kahan, also with the Cultural Cognition Project.[145] He says that if the implications of the information in question – say, the need for more government-imposed restrictions on bitumen development, if not an outright moratorium, or the need to reduce carbon emissions to prevent the devastating impacts of climate change – if those things affirm your values, you're willing to accept that information more readily. But if the information presented to you doesn't affirm your values, then you're likely to reject it altogether, no matter how compelling the evidence.

This, in large part, is why Michael Marx brought in an ad agency to help an international network of citizen and indigenous groups raise the stakes in the Great Bitumen War. "There needed to be costs," he said, "for Alberta to respond to criticism simply with public relations."[146]

What Marx and his group unleashed in the summer of 2010 became the most controversial campaign against tar sands development. They called the project Rethink Alberta, and the goal, said Marx, was to make the Alberta government pay for the fact that it was allowing the irresponsible development of its tar sands. "The Alberta government indicated that its brand was important to it. We've learned that everybody has to protect their brand, so we decided to go after their brand with the threat of a tourism boycott. This was a shot across the bow to encourage the government to sit down with stakeholders to figure out how to manage the tar sands properly."[147]

Relentless media coverage of the devastating effects of the BP oil spill in the Gulf of Mexico ensured that the potential destructiveness of oil production was fresh in everyone's mind. So Marx and the ad agency designed a campaign comparing tar sands development to the BP disaster. Billboards sprouted in large American and British cities, and a TV-commercial-like video spread like a virus around the Internet, parts of it even appearing on major news networks. The video begins with a lyrical and romanticized depiction of the most beautiful parts of Alberta, mostly the snow-capped mountains on the province's western edge, the same images used by the Alberta government to promote tourism: the purity of snow-white glaciers, canoeing across the tranquil waters of a pristine lake, riders galloping their horses through the rolling foothills. A gentle female voice tells us,

"Thousands of bird species live peacefully amongst bear cubs and bumblebees." Suddenly, images of Alberta's bitumen mines and belching upgraders intrude and eventually take over the screen. A concerned and foreboding voice-over accompanies footage of oil-soaked ducks struggling to stay afloat in a tailings pond.

"Think you know Alberta?" the narrator intones darkly. "Think again."

A litany of facts are presented in the film and listed on the Rethink Alberta website, most of them in keeping with those on Pembina's website. The tailings ponds are toxic and they do leak; thousands of birds have flown into them and drowned or died of ingested poisons. The mines and upgraders look like the trappings of Tolkien's Mordor, and development likely will drive caribou populations extinct. Native communities living downstream suffer from increased rates of rare cancers and other diseases linked to the same toxic compounds found in tar sands production, a concern that experts claim deserves further study to see if the toxins and the cancers are linked. Alberta is obsessed with wealth at the expense of the environment and people, and that the tar sands threaten to keep the US, Asia and Europe addicted to oil for many more decades.

Some of the facts cited by Rethink Alberta, however, are questionable. The initial version of the video claimed that the area of forest that could be destroyed or degraded was twice the size of England, which is just plain wrong. After howls of protest from the Alberta government and CAPP – this is one of those outrageous falsehoods on Janet Annesley's Top 10 list – the video's creators admitted to an editing error. They immediately changed it to the accurate figure – the size of just one England, which is still a fair chunk of real estate similar in size to Iowa or New York – and reposted the video.

The narrator also suggests that tar sands development "could result in the loss of millions of migratory birds and other wildlife," a claim apparently based on a report called *Danger in the Nursery* issued by the Natural Resource Defense Council.[148] This is definitely an example of unsubstantiated bullshit. In an op-ed published in the *Edmonton Journal*, ecologist Kevin Timoney, a fierce critic of Alberta's management of bitumen development and one of the report's peer reviewers, pointed out, among other errors, that the report "assumed that peak [bird] landing rates exist 24 hours per day for 100 days."[149] In reality, he wrote, peak landing rates only happen during migration, which lasts only one to three weeks each year.

Timoney later did his own analysis, with Dalhousie University biologist Robert Ronconi, and found that bird deaths were likely much higher than those reported by industry but not nearly as high as claimed by NRDC. Their study estimated that between 458 and 5,029 birds die each year after landing on tailings ponds, compared to just 65 reported by industry.[150] "We presented a range rather than a particular value, to emphasize the point that mortality is quite variable over space and time," explained Timoney, who used three data sets for his study. "There is no systematic, scientifically defensible monitoring of the tailings pond," Timoney told Edmonton journalist Jodie Sinnema. "The industry will tell you that they monitor, but it's really ad hoc. It's a person who may notice a duck dead along the road and may or may not report it. There's no research team that sits there and goes out repeatedly in a scientifically defensible, statistically robust manner to assess the number of birds dying. So you could have a mortality event that's entirely missed and of course that would underestimate the mortality."[151]

Timoney said he discussed the flawed methodology with the NRDC report's main author, but the latter evidently chose to ignore that advice. The fact that the author disregarded Timoney's concerns, and that NRDC went ahead and published the report anyway, indicates that in this case there was a lack of connection to a concern with truth. Mark Evans might call it "rubbish" for its deficiency in factual grounding, or "irretrievable speculation" for the "crucial lack of any plausible means of verification."[152] Either way, it is clear that NRDC and Corporate Ethics International were trying to exaggerate the tar sands' deadly impact on birds. The same could be said for Michael Marx's claim that Alberta's bitumen experiment is "the most environmentally destructive energy project on earth," given the impacts of mountaintop-removal coal mining and some mega-hydro projects. But if bitumen exploitation is allowed to continue as planned, his claim may well come true.

The rest of the material in the Rethink Alberta video certainly paints Alberta's bitumen development, and the politicians who have sanctioned it, in a negative light, but it is difficult to call it bullshit. True, there is no mention of the fact that industry has made great strides in reducing GHG intensity per barrel of oil, or that a small portion of the landscape that has been disturbed has been restored to some modest level of ecological function. But these selective "facts" that were omitted are virtually irrelevant in the context of the scope and scale of the tar sands, especially when compared to the Triple Alliance's refusal to acknowledge the social and environmental impacts, the uncertainties and risks, that scientific research indicates are very real.

Not surprisingly in this high-stakes battle, the response to Rethink Alberta was swift and fierce. Editorial boards and columnists condemned the campaign for trying to undermine Alberta's tourism economy. CAPP too attacked the group with the vigour of a pit bull. "We suggest to Corporate Ethics International the only ethical response is a full correction to their ads, website and statements to media," Janet Annesley told an industry-friendly publication called *Energize Alberta*. "Our research indicates that Canadians want a more balanced discussion than activist groups have so far provided," she continued, apparently without irony. "Saying 'Stop the fill-in-the-blank' over and over with no realistic energy or economic solutions offered is a message that appeals to people's environmental concerns but does not recognize our needs also for energy and economic growth."[153]

Annesley's response represents a common practice in the public relations world. Instead of acknowledging and addressing the legitimate social and environmental issues raised by Corporate Ethics International and other environmental groups, the brains behind CAPP's own advertising campaign simply refocused the debate elsewhere. Annesley accused Corporate Ethics International of unethical behaviour and then deftly skirted the environmental issues raised by Rethink Alberta and, right on message, deflected the conversation toward the environmentalists' failure to reconfigure our entire energy economy in the face of strident opposition from the very industry she represents.

For Marx, such diversionary tactics are simply part of a large and complex strategy that has allowed the Triple Alliance to win battle after battle in the global war over the future of oil.

Despite enhanced public concern and awareness, and despite increasing scientific evidence of the enormous risks to the local environment and the global climate, tar sands development continues to proceed at a breakneck pace. At the same time, scientific evidence continues to mount that if we are to keep global warming below the 2°C threshold the international community has agreed to, then we need to stop developing and burning not only tar sands oil, but all oil, coal and natural gas as quickly as possible. We are running out of time, but political will and the profiteering oil industry are not changing fast enough to prevent what most climate scientists concede is a monumental, and probably disastrous, warming of our climate. This, Marx maintains, more than justifies his public-relations approach to combatting the tar sands problem, and he warns Canadians that they should expect more of such measures in the future:

> I see everything in terms of a continuum,
> where everything is exactly factual at
> one end and everything is totally false
> and manipulative at the other end. We
> say, "They're destroying an area the size of

England." In our mind, they are in the process of destroying an area the size of England. Is that the most persuasive way? Yes. Is that what Pembina would say? No. But in my mind, we are to the truthful side of the centre point. We're engaged in persuasion. That's exactly what *they* do: they're on the other side of the [centre point]. [Industry and government] put the best slant on the facts for them, and we're putting the best slant on the facts for us. Like them, we're in the business of persuasion. Is it truthful? Yes. Is it balanced? No. But we're not trying to be balanced. We're trying to be persuasive.[154]

Since Rethink Alberta launched in 2010, the anti-environmentalist rhetoric has intensified to fever pitch. Government documents made public through an access-to-information request in early 2012 indicated that the Harper Conservatives considered environmental organizations (and Aboriginal groups) as "adversaries," while industry associations, energy companies and the National Energy Board – which is supposed to be an independent body that evaluates new projects, such as Enbridge's Northern Gateway pipeline across central British Columbia – enjoyed the status of "allies."[155]

A week after the documents were made public, the federal Conservatives publicly labelled Aboriginal and environmental groups as "radicals" and "extremists."[156] Politicians deny it, of course, but if there is any truth in former Forest Ethics communications manager Andrew Frank's sworn affidavit, Harper's bureaucrats are roaming the countryside, trying to intimidate those who fund environmental organizations and branding certain groups and individuals as "enemies" of the government and of the people of Canada.[157]

Branding the other side as an enemy is a ploy the Republican Party in the US has used with great success over the last 20 years. GOP politicians routinely demonize Democrats and other liberals. Newt Gingrich issued a now infamous memo to fellow conservatives about the words they should use to describe liberals: abuse of power, betray, bizarre, corrupt, criminal rights, cheat, devour, disgrace, greed, steal, sick, traitors, radical, red tape, unionized, waste welfare. "The words and phrases are powerful," he wrote. "Read them. Memorize as many as possible. And remember that, like any tool, these words will not help if they are not used."

Moral philosopher Jonathan Haidt is concerned about the fallout from this kind of political rhetoric. While he says that "groupish tribalism" is something humans evolved with, and is a normal and healthy part of social dynamics, some situations can exacerbate our innate us-versus-them mentality. For instance, he says, nothing gets a nation together like a foreign attack, something the US saw with Pearl Harbor and 9-11. But even when there are no external attacks, moral divisions within the group can ramp up tribalism to "pathological proportions."

> The tribalism evolved, ultimately, for war. And when it reaches a certain intensity, the switch is flipped and the other side is evil. They're not just our opponents, they're evil. And once you think they're evil, then the ends justify the means. And you can break laws and you can do anything, because it's in the service of fighting evil.

Tribalism also forces people to choose sides,

and most of us want to be with the "good" people. Baby boomers, says Haidt, are more prone to "Manichaean thinking" and quick to choose one side or the other. (Manichaeus, also called Mani, was a third-century Persian prophet who preached that the world is a battleground between the forces of light and the forces of darkness.)

"Of course, we all believe that we have sided with good," Haidt continued, "but that means that the other people have sided with evil.... and when it gets to the mental state in which I am fighting for good and you are fighting for evil, it's very difficult to compromise. Compromise becomes a dirty word."[158]

Critics of Harper's Manichaean strategy over environmental issues came out swinging, of course, concerned that it might lead to an all-out assault on the rights and freedoms of those who oppose oil sands development. "Efforts by Prime Minister Stephen Harper and his natural resources minister to characterize charitable organizations as dangerous radicals assaulting the national interest is far removed from the truth," wrote Alan Broadbent in a *Globe and Mail* op-ed. Broadbent is chairman and CEO of Avana Capital Corp., chairman of the Maytree Foundation and a board member of Tides Canada Foundation, one of the funders federal bureaucrats tried to intimidate. "Such dubious claims reflect either a willful ignorance of the truth or a willingness to bend it to favour their own interests."[159]

The damage was done, however. The Triple Alliance, of which the Harper Conservatives are an integral part, once again had shifted the debate in its favour by branding tar sands opponents as evil traitors; by implication, this left tar sands supporters as virtuous defenders of Canada's best interests. The *Calgary Herald* editorial board even had the temerity to blame the "eco-pests" who signed up to testify at the National Energy Board's hearings on the Northern Gateway pipeline for the Conservatives' ideologically motivated attempt to weaken Canada's already abysmal Environmental Assessment Act.[160]

Some environmentalists, even those who oppose the expansion of the tar sands, have been critical of the move toward public relations and away from science-based facts. A friend of mine, a conservationist oilman who suggested I not use the term "tar sands" in this book, almost froths

at the mouth when he hears environmental organizations "exaggerating" the impacts of tar sands
development when "there are so many other, more
important issues to deal with." When I suggest
that the industry he works for is as or more guilty
of overstating the benefits and ignoring the costs
and risks of their activities, he says he holds environmentalists, who largely have been focused on
getting the facts straight, to a higher standard.

Bob Gibson, a professor of environmental
studies at the University of Waterloo, admonishes
environmentalists for embellishment, omissions
and other forms of bullshit as much as he does
the cornucopian politicians and industrialists
who have perfected the art. "Their battles for
influence based on swayed opinion threaten to
bury the struggle for truthful communication,
perhaps even truthful understanding," he wrote
in *Alternatives Journal*. "[D]eserving of celebra-
tion, however, are the activists who refuse to stoop.
There is nothing easier today than to step down
into the trough and fight one-sided bullshit with
other-sided bullshit. Maybe sometimes the green
poop will prevail, but the smell remains and the
substance is corrosive."[161]

Gibson is right to decry the pre-eminence of propaganda in all its manifestations in public discourse. But given all the evidence – the ineffectual regulatory system in Canada, the lack of progress on reducing GHG emissions, and the human tendency to ignore scientific evidence in favour of the status quo – what choice does the environmental community really have? Stay committed to repeating the facts, and, like the British redcoats who refused to change their traditional tactics in the American War of Independence, lose the battle? Or incorporate the best public-relations strategies they can afford on their meagre budgets while maintaining an earnest concern for and connection to the truth?

George Hoberg, an American-born political scientist at the University of British Columbia, has wrestled with this conundrum and drawn similar conclusions in relation to the climate change debate. Posting to his *GreenPolicyProf* blog,[162] he wrote:

> As an academic, I've always prided myself
> on the commitment to analytical reason
> and been uncomfortable with the rhetoric

of advocates even when I've shared their values. But in recent years I've felt increasingly unsettled in that stance as the gravity of the climate crisis has become more apparent. The past two decades of climate politics have clearly demonstrated that "speaking truth to power" has not been effective at inspiring climate action. And as I've tried to come to a deeper understanding about humanity's failure to act yet on climate change, I came to an insight that transformed my stance.

When you consider the structure of the climate challenge as a public goods and public choice dilemma, you can see that if we are guided by short-term material thinking, we will simply be incapable of rising to the challenge of taking the concerted action sufficient to avoid dangerous climate change. The logic of the climate policy analyst is dominated by this economic rationality that can't generate the necessary solutions. To envision a capacity to act you need to take a leap of faith that enough citizens and leaders are willing to act on moral, not economic,

> grounds. You take climate action not because
> it is in your or your nation's interests, but
> because it is the right thing to do. And you
> need to start acting that way yourself.

Hoberg recounts a conversation he had with author and climate activist Bill McKibben, one of America's finest contemporary environmental writers and a professor at Middlebury College in Vermont. McKibben wrote *The End of Nature* (1989), the first popular book about the disastrous implications of climate change, and many other books and articles about the serious environmental issues we face. Confronted with the dire consequences his research uncovered, McKibben became an outspoken advocate about the need to fix the climate problem. He is also a fierce opponent of the continued development of Alberta's tar sands.

When McKibben visited UBC to give a speech, Hoberg challenged him on some of the factual inconsistencies in his rhetoric. Hoberg found McKibben to be cognizant of the problems inherent in relying on facts alone to win the debate, and wrote that McKibben "bemoaned analysts who were "in love with the caveat" and unwilling to join hands with advocates in the fight for climate action. He explained that he was sensitive to the concerns of many academics that they would be sacrificing their credibility if they engaged in advocacy. He then spoke of the gravity of the climate crisis, calling it the "greatest challenge of our time," and asked, "What are you saving your credibility for?"

Hoberg, like McKibben, has realized that facts alone are not enough. If we're going to reduce and eventually eliminate our reliance on fossil fuels, and solve the numerous environmental problems caused by industrial-scale natural resource exploitation, we're going to need to build a strong political movement that results in meaningful government action. "By taking on a more explicit advocacy role," Hoberg argues, "I'm not abandoning the commitment to analytic rigour typified by the logic of the analyst. I see myself as harnessing that in the service of advocacy."

What Michael Marx and the rest of the environmental community are trying to do is show us the dark side of the tar sands – the one we'd prefer to ignore if we could, and the one government and industry either ignore or actively misrepresent in their "Tell It Like It Is" truth campaigns. Although our minds seem to rest easier if we embrace their version of the truth as we go about our daily routines, it is our obligation as citizens in a democratic society to challenge them at every turn. As George Orwell so famously reminded us more than half a century ago, all issues are political issues, and politics itself is a mass of lies, evasions and folly. We must take the time to assay these competing interpretations of reality and take a stand on what kind of world we want future generations – our children and grandchildren – to live in.

Conservative politicians and the oil industry will not relent in their ideological and self-interested war on truth as they continue to promote the extraction and combustion of every last drop of oil on the planet. They will deny the death of the old order, and they will only change if we make them change. To do that, we must take responsibility for the little black lies we tell ourselves. We need to take our role as citizens seriously and examine not only the "facts" of any given controversy but the integrity of our own values, which will ultimately decide the trajectory of the future.

The Great Bitumen War seems to indicate that a paternalistic, top-down power structure bent on entrenching the questionable efficacy of fundamentalist free enterprise is doomed to fail us. At the same time, it is inconceivable that we can solve the social, economic and environmental challenges before us without the active role of government regulation and oversight to tap and direct the undeniable power of commerce and industry.

The ability of our democratic societies to have an open and honest conversation about how to effectively and efficiently govern the marketplace – and thus limit and redress the environmental problems before us – will require all of us to open our eyes and forsake the self-imposed innocence we cling to like a life preserver in an ocean of uncertainty. These are challenging times, but it is our obligation to re-examine the beliefs that threaten to undermine the fabric of our societies and the natural world on which they depend. After all, we are not born the monsters James Baldwin so feared, but we can become them all too easily. Thankfully, the individual freedoms sanctified by our democracies allow us – indeed obligate us – to mould the world and ourselves in any number of different ways, a luxury most of our fellow human beings in places like China and Russia do not enjoy. This ongoing process of re-creation, however, must be based on an unequivocal regard for the truth and an absolute abhorrence for bullshit in all its insidious manifestations.

Because a future built on little black lies will be a dark one indeed.

Key References and Additional Reading

Ayles, G. Burton, et al. *Oil Sands Regional Aquatic Monitoring Program (RAMP) Scientific Peer Review of the Five Year Report (1997–2001)*. Edmonton: February 13, 2004, PDF accessed July 15, 2012. www.andrewnikiforuk.com/page2/ page2.html at linked document "RAMP Peer Review."

Bernays, Edward. *Propaganda*. New York: Horace Liveright, 1928.

Boyd, David. *Unnatural Law: Rethinking Canadian Environmental Law and Policy*. Vancouver: UBC Press, 2003.

British Broadcasting Corporation. *Century of the Self*. Video documentary (4:00:00) aired on BBC Four April 29–May 7, 2002. Accessed July 31, 2012. YouTube. http://is.gd/o2pGQF.

Canadian Association of Petroleum Producers. "Canada's Industry. Oil Sands."Accessed June 22, 2012. www.capp.ca/ canadaindustry/oilsands/Pages/default.aspx.

Canadian Broadcasting Corporation Documentaries. *Tipping Point: The Age of the Oil Sands*. Written and directed by Tom Radford and Niobe Thompson of Clearwater Media in association with CBC-TV et al., 2010, aired on CBC's *The Nature of Things* January 27, 2011. Video accessed August 2, 2012. http://is.gd/I1mApv.

Canadian Environmental Assessment Act, S.C. 1992, c. 37. Full text (HTML) accessed August 1, 2012. http://canlii.ca/t/kwcj. [Please see also note 98 as to CEAA 2012.]

Chen, Yiqun. *Cancer Incidence in Fort Chipewyan, Alberta: 1995–2006.* Edmonton: Alberta Cancer Board, February 2009. PDF accessed July 15, 2012. www.albertahealthservices.ca/500.asp.

Corporate Ethics International. Rethink Alberta. Accessed June 22, 2012. www.rethinkalberta.com/main.php.

Dembicki, Geoff. "War Over Oil Sands: Report from Washington, DC" series. *The Tyee,* March 14–April 7, 2011. Accessed April 15, 2012. http://thetyee.ca/Series/2011/03/15/WarOverOilSands.

DeSmogBlog. Search "oilsands." Accessed April 15, 2012. www.desmogblog.com/search/node/oilsands.

Dillon, Peter, et al. *Evaluation of Four Reports on Contamination of the Athabasca River System by Oil Sands Operations.* Edmonton: Water Monitoring Data Review Committee for Alberta Environment, 2011. Backgrounder and PDF accessed August 2, 2012. http://environment.alberta.ca/03183.html.

Dowdeswell, Liz, et al. *A Foundation for the Future: Building an Environmental Monitoring System for the Oil Sands.* Ottawa: Environment Canada, 2010.

Evernden, Neil. *The Natural Alien.* Toronto: University of Toronto Press, 1993.

Frankfurt, Harry. *On Bullshit.* Princeton, N.J.: Princeton University Press, 2005.

Government of Alberta. Alberta's Oil Sands. "Alberta. Tell it like it is." Accessed May 8, 2011. www.oilsands.alberta.ca/tellitlikeitis.html.

Grant, Jennifer, et al. *Solving the Puzzle: Environmental Responsibility in Oilsands Development.* Calgary: Pembina Institute, 2011.

Griffiths, Mary, Amy Taylor and Dan Woynillowicz. *Troubled Waters, Troubling Trends: Technology and Policy Options To Reduce Water Use in Oil and Oilsands Development in Alberta.* Calgary: Pembina Institute, 2006.

Hardcastle, Gary L., and George A. Reisch, eds. *Bullshit and Philosophy: Guaranteed To Get Perfect Results Every Time.* Chicago: Open Court, 2006.

Hoberg, George. "The Three Logics of Climate Politics." *GreenPolicyProf* blog. February 13, 2012. Accessed June 22, 2012. http://greenpolicyprof.org/wordpress/?p=790.

Hoggan, James. *Climate Cover-up: The Crusade to Deny Global Warming.* Vancouver: Greystone Books, 2009.

Hrudey, Steve, et al. *Environmental and Health Impacts of Canada's Oil Sands Industry.* Ottawa: Royal Society of Canada, 2010. PDF accessed August 2, 2012, www.rsc.ca/creports.php.

Kahan, Dan M., Hank Jenkins-Smith and Donald Braman. "Cultural Cognition of Scientific Consensus." *Journal of Risk Research* 14 (2011): 147–74. Full text (PDF) accessed August 1, 2012. http://dx.doi.org/10.2139/ssrn.1549444.

Kelly, Erin, et al. "Oil sands development contributes elements toxic at low concentrations to the Athabasca River and its tributaries." *Proceedings of the National Academy of Sciences of the United States of America* 107, no. 37 (2010): 16178–83. Full text (HTML) accessed August 1, 2012. www.pnas.org/content/107/37/16178.full.

———."Oil sands development contributes polycyclic aromatic compounds to the Athabasca River and its tributaries." *Proceedings of the National Academy of Sciences of the United States of America* 106, no. 52 (2009): 22346–51. Full text (HTML) accessed August 1, 2012. www.pnas.org/content/106/52/22346.full.

Kunda, Ziva. "The Case for Motivated Reasoning." *Psychological Bulletin* 108, no. 3 (1990): 480–98. Full text (PDF) accessed August 4, 2012. http://is.gd/avQCdA.

Leach, Andrew. *Rescuing the Frog* blog. http://andrewleach.ca.

Leiss, William. "How Canada's Stumbles with Environmental Risk Management Reflect an Integrity Gap." In *The Integrity Gap: Canada's Environmental Policy and Institutions*, edited by Eugene Lee and Anthony Perl. Vancouver: UBC Press, 2003.

Levi, Michael A. *The Canadian Oil Sands: Energy Security vs. Climate Change.* New York: Council on Foreign Relations Press, 2009.

Main, Catherine, et al. *2010 Regional Aquatics Monitoring Program (RAMP) Scientific Review.* Calgary: Alberta Innovates, 2011.

Moorhouse, Jeremy, Danielle Droitsch and Dan Woynillowicz. *Life Cycle Assessments of Oilsands Greenhouse Gas Emissions.*

Calgary: Pembina Institute, 2011. PDF accessed August 4, 2012. www.pembina.org/pub/2163.

National Task Force on Oilsands Strategy. *The Oilsands: A New Energy Vision for Canada.* Edmonton: Alberta Chamber of Resources, 1995.

Nikiforuk, Andrew. *Tar Sands: Dirty Oil and the Future of a Continent.* Revised and updated edition. Vancouver: Greystone Books, 2010.

Office of the Auditor General of Canada. *2011 October Report of the Commissioner of the Environment and Sustainable Development.* Accessed August 1, 2012. http://is.gd/T6hwSo.

Oreskes, Naomi, and Erik Conway. *Merchants of Doubt: How a Handful of Scientists Obscured the Truth on Issues from Tobacco Smoke to Global Warming.* New York: Bloomsbury Press, 2010.

Pembina Institute. OilSandsWatch.org.

Proctor, Robert, and Londa Schiebinger, eds. *Agnotology: The Making and Unmaking of Ignorance.* Stanford, Calif.: Stanford University Press, 2008.

Schindler, David. "Tar sands needs solid science." *Nature* 468 (November 25, 2010): 499–501. Citation accessed August 2, 2012. www.nature.com/nature/journal/v468/n7323/full/468499a.html.

Stauber, John C., and Sheldon Rampton. *Toxic Sludge Is Good for You: Lies, Damn Lies and the Public Relations Industry.* Monroe, Me.: Common Courage Press, 1995.

Swart, Neil S., and Andrew Weaver. "The Alberta oil sands and climate." *Nature Climate Change* 2, no. 3 (March 2012, print): 134–36. Citation accessed May 30, 2012. http://is.gd/XO8oBV.

Timoney, Kevin, and Peter Lee. "Polycyclic aromatic hydrocarbons increase in Athabasca River delta sediment: Temporal trends and environmental correlates." *Environmental Science & Technology* 45, no. 10 (April 26, 2011): 4278–84. Abstract accessed August 1, 2012. http://pubs.acs.org/doi/abs/10.1021/es104375d.

Wells, Jeff, et al. *Danger in the Nursery: Impact on Birds of Tar Sands Oil Development in Canada's Boreal Forest.* New York: Natural Resources Defense Council, 2008.

Notes

What's in a Name?

1 Neil Evernden, *The Natural Alien* (Toronto: University of
Toronto Press, 1993): 145.

2 as to relative quantities of reserves:
Canadian Association of Petroleum Producers, *Upstream
Dialogue: The Facts on Oil Sands* (June 2012): 10 (PDF
accessed July 31, 2012. www.capp.ca/UpstreamDialogue/
OilSands/Pages/default.aspx;

as to world rank of Canada's reserves:
Oil Sands Developers Group, Responsible Oil Sands
Development, "Oil Sands Facts," http://is.gd/xpqxQE;
U.S. Energy Information Administration, *International
Energy Outlook 2011*, Report no. DOE/EIA-0484
(September 19, 2011): 38, Table 5, PDF accessed July 31, 2012,
www.eia.gov/forecasts/ieo.

3 Alberta Energy Resources Conservation Board, *ST98-2012:
Alberta's Energy Reserves 2011 and Supply/Demand Outlook
2012–2021* (June 2012): §3.2.1, p3-16 (PDF p86), Fig 3.26,
p3-23 (PDF p97), accessed August 4, 2012, www.ercb.ca/sts/
ST98/ST98-2012.pdf.

4   Yiqun Chen, "Cancer Incidence in Fort Chipewyan,
    Alberta: 1995–2006" (Edmonton: Alberta Cancer Board,
    February 2009): 13ff, PDF accessed July 15, 2012, www.
    albertahealthservices.ca/500.asp.

5   "No to a new tar sands pipeline,"*New York Times* editorial,
    April 2, 2011, WK9, full text accessed July 31, 2012, www.
    nytimes.com/2011/04/03/opinion/03sun1.html (registra-
    tion may be required for access).

6   Sheldon Alberts, "Obama voices oilsands concern,"
    Calgary Herald, April 6, 2011, A1, accessed August 1,
    2012, Calgary Public Library, http://calgarypubliclibrary.
    com/books-more/e-library?s=94, Canadian Newsstand,
    ProQuest document ID 861117384 (CPL card number and
    password required for database access; please consult your
    local library as to availability of this resource).

7   "It's no pipe dream; politics has no place in Keystone
    review," *Calgary Herald*, April 10, 2011, A9, accessed
    August 3, 2012, through public library as specified in note
    6, Canadian Newsstand,ProQuest document ID 861514661;
    see also:

    Peter Foster, "All the hysteria that's fit to print," *National
    Post*, April 5, 2011, FP11, Canadian Newsstand, ProQuest
    document ID 860887255.

8   Ed Stelmach, "Canadian oil is important" (Edmonton:
    Office of the Premier of Alberta, n.d., scanned full text on
    letterhead (PDF) accessed July 30, 2012, www.bilateralist.
    com/2011/04/07/stelmach-ny-times-pipeline-jobs-jobs-jobs
    [NB: no letter from Ed Stelmach could be found at nytimes.
    com]; *but see*:

Russ Girling, April 7, 2011, letter to *NYT* re editorial cited
above in note 5, accessed July 30, 2012, www.nytimes.
com/2011/04/08/opinion/l08pipeline.html (registration
may be required; alternatively, search "Russ Girling" at
nytimes.com main page).

9 CAPP, "Oil Sands or Tar Sands?" n.d., in comment section
"Your Feedback to CAPP," accessed May 6, 2011, www.capp.
ca/canadaIndustry/oilSands/Energy-Economy/Pages/
OilSands-or-TarSands.aspx.

10 See, for example, *The Oil Sands: A New Energy Vision for
Canada* (Edmonton: Alberta Chamber of Resources, 1995),
PDF accessed July 30, 2012, http://is.gd/Qssonz; *see also*, as
to "yogurt," note 79 below and:

Kevin Libin, "Emerging oil-sands ad battle getting
personal," *National Post*, December 2, 2010, accessed
August 1, 2012, http://is.gd/fhXzaa;
as to "peanut butter,"

CAPP, "In situ extraction of bitumen that's as clean as
conventional" (n.d.), quoting Eddie Lui of Imperial Oil,
accessed August 1, 2012, http://is.gd/L2IdU5.

11 For the whole story on the rebranding of the Patagonian
toothfish, read Bruce Knecht's *Hooked: Pirates, Poaching
and the Perfect Fish* (Emmaus, Pa.: Rodale Books, 2006).

12 Tom Brokaw, "Brokaw explores the vanishing Chilean sea
bass," MSNBC (n.d.), accessed May 6, 2011, http://today.
msnbc.msn.com/id/12939001/ns/today-books.

13 Paula Arab, "Language tars debate over Alberta oilsands,"
Calgary Herald, April 21, 2011, A14, accessed August

3, 2012, through public library as specified in note 6, Canadian Newsstand, ProQuest document ID 863060637.

14 Facebook page for CBC British Columbia's *Early Edition*, responding to a query from listener Andrew Smith, n.d., accessed July 30, 2012, http://is.gd/oFUUfj;

   see also the revised and updated edition of Nikiforuk's *Tar Sands* (Vancouver: Greystone Books 2010) for the most encyclopedic and up-to-date critique of Canadian policy and practice related to bitumen extraction and production.

Not All Facts Are Equal

15 *As It Happens*, CBC Radio, September 29, 2011, "Obit: Pierre Dansereau," transcript of an 04:06 program segment beginning at ~10:30 in streaming audio Part Three, with quoted words from 1972 Massey Lecture at ~12:15, accessed May 30, 2012, http://is.gd/cvI5Np.

16 "Alberta buys $56k ad in US paper," CBC News, July 2, 2010, accessed July 15, 2012, http://is.gd/XD2eow.

17 Government of Alberta, Alberta's Oil Sands, "Alberta. Tell it like it is," n.d., accessed May 8, 2011, www.oilsands. alberta.ca/tellitlikeitis.html.

18 Pembina Institute, OilSandsWatch.org, "Tailings," n.d., accessed July 30, 2012, www.pembina.org/oil-sands/os101/ tailings. For accurate and independent facts about the scope and impacts of bitumen operations in Alberta, I recommend OilSandsWatch.org; *see also*, e.g.,

Ed Struzik, "Killing wolves: A product of Alberta's big oil and gas boom," October 27, 2011, Yale Environment360, accessed August 4, 2012, http://is.gd/zmmUms.

19 Pembina, OilSandsWatch.org, "Climate Impacts," n.d., accessed May 30, 2012, http://is.gd/C4bNfP.

20 Regional Aquatics Monitoring Program, n.d., accessed July 15, 2012, www.ramp-alberta.org/ramp.aspx.

21 Ibid.

22 Alberta Premier Ed Stelmach speech to Alberta Enterprise Group Energy Forum, Washington, DC, January 16, 2008, quoted in Greenpeace, "Government Fiction vs. Tar Sands Facts," n.d., p1, col. 1 of PDF accessed August 4, 2012, http://dirtyoilsands.org/files/Gov.FictionVS_.TSFacts_.pdf; *see also*:

"Forum Speaking Notes: Hon. Ed Stelmach, Premier of Alberta," MSWord text accessed August 2, 2012, www.gwest.net/documents/PremierStelmachAlbertaEnterpriseGroupEnergyForum.doc.

23 "Oilsands pollution findings conflict: Prentice," CBC News Edmonton, September 1, 2010, accessed May 30, 2012, http://is.gd/p5yncS.

24 Andrew Nikiforuk, "Alberta still wears pollution blinders: Report," *The Tyee*, February 1, 2011, accessed May 30, 2012, http://is.gd/NuyfdJ.

25 Pembina Institute, OilSandsWatch.org, "Alberta's Oilsands," n.d., accessed August 3, 2012, www.pembina.org/oil-sands/os101/alberta; *see also*:

Government of Alberta, Alberta's Oil Sands, "Reclamation," accessed May 8, 2011, www.oilsands.alberta. ca/reclamation.html.

26 Pembina Institute, OilSandsWatch.org, "Tailings," n.d., accessed July 30, 2012, www.pembina.org/oil-sands/os101/ tailings; *see also*, as to extent of territory suitable for in situ extraction, Pembina page cited in note 25.

27 David Schindler, personal communication with the author, March 11, 2012.

28 Ibid.

29 *See* Yiqun Chen as cited above in note 4; as to federal review of RAMP, *see* Ayles et al. as cited below in note 42.

30 Several peer-reviewed studies have indicated that industrial exploitation of Alberta's bitumen deposits is releasing toxins into the regional environment. *See*, e.g.:

Erin Kelly et al., "Oil sands development contributes polycyclic aromatic compounds to the Athabasca River and its tributaries," *Proceedings of the National Academy of Sciences* 106, no. 52 (December 29, 2009): 22346–51, full text (HTML) accessed August 1, 2012, www.pnas.org/ content/106/52/22346.full;

———."Oil sands development contributes elements toxic at low concentrations to the Athabasca River and its tributaries," *PNAS* 107, no. 37 (September 14, 2010): 16178–83, full text (HTML) accessed August 1, 2012, www. pnas.org/content/107/37/16178.full; and

Kevin Timoney and Peter Lee, "Polycyclic aromatic hydrocarbons increase in Athabasca River delta sediment: Temporal trends and environmental correlates," *Environmental Science & Technology* 45, no. 10 (April 26, 2011): 4278–84, abstract accessed August 1, 2012, http://pubs.acs.org/doi/abs/10.1021/es104375d.

31 Andrew Nikiforuk, "Oil sands pollute with fish-killing toxins, new study shows," *The Tyee*, August 30, 2010, accessed May 30, 2012, http://thetyee.ca/News/2010/08/30/TarSandsStudy.

32 David Schindler, personal communication with the author, March 11, 2012.

33 *Tipping Point: The Age of the Oil Sands,*" at ~1:15:00 in 1:30:00 documentary film written and directed by Tom Radford and Niobe Thompson of Clearwater Media in association with CBC-TV et al., 2010, aired on CBC's *The Nature of Things* January 27, 2011, video accessed August 2, 2012, www.cbc.ca/documentaries/natureofthings/2011/tippingpoint; *see also* http://tippingpointdoc.ca re theatrical and DVD release as *Tipping Point: The End of Oil*, with narration by Sigourney Weaver.

34 Andrew Nikiforuk, "A smoking gun on Athabasca River: Deformed fish," *The Tyee*, September 17, 2010, accessed August 2, 2012, at http://is.gd/hyp1JC.

35 "Oilsands water toxins natural, monitor says," CBC TV News, August 31, 2010, video accessed May 30, 2012, http://is.gd/qg0Kf7.

36 "Oilsands pollution findings conflict: Prentice," CBC News
    Edmonton, September 1, 2010, accessed March 20, 2012,
    http://is.gd/p5yncS.

37 *Tipping Point* from ~1:20:40.

38 David Schindler, personal communication with the author,
    March 11, 2012.

39 Andrew Nikiforuk, "Series of reports blacken oil sands
    managers," *The Tyee*, December 22, 2010, accessed May 30,
    2012, http://is.gd/g3Trd8.

40 Darcy Henton, "Ministers hail 'world-leading' monitoring,"
    Calgary Herald, February 4, 2012, A1, accessed August
    3, 2012, through public library as specified in note 6,
    Canadian Newsstand, ProQuest document ID 920030529.

41 Alberta Environment, July 8, 1996, backgrounder and full
    text (HTML) accessed August 1, 2012, www3.gov.ab.ca/env/
    water/nrbs/nrbs.html.

42 Several independent scientific reviews have been conducted
    recently on the effectiveness and adequacy of government
    and industry monitoring programs in the Athabasca oil
    sands region. Although government and industry have
    interpreted these reports in the most positive light possible,
    the results indicate that current monitoring programs are
    grossly inadequate. *See*, e.g.:

    G. Burton Ayles et al., *Oil Sands Regional Aquatic
    Monitoring Program (RAMP) Scientific Peer Review of the
    Five Year Report (1997–2001)*, submitted to RAMP Steering
    Committee February 13, 2004, PDF accessed July 15, 2012,

www.andrewnikiforuk.com/page2/page2.html at linked
document "RAMP Peer Review";

Liz Dowdeswell et al., *A Foundation for the Future:
Building an Environmental Monitoring System for the Oil
Sands* (Ottawa: Environment Canada, 2010), full text
(HTML) accessed July 15, 2012,http://is.gd/hNcTV4;

Steve Hrudey et al., *Environmental and Health Impacts of
Canada's Oil Sands Industry* as cited in note 98 below.

Catherine Main et al., *2010 Regional Aquatics Monitoring
Program (RAMP) Scientific Review* (Calgary: Alberta
Innovates, 2011), PDF accessed August 2, 2012, http://
is.gd/4wcpis at subhead "The final report..."; and

Peter Dillon et al., *Evaluation of Four Reports on
Contamination of the Athabasca River System by Oil Sands
Operations*, prepared for Alberta Environment by Water
Monitoring Data Review Committee March 7, 2011,
backgrounder and PDF accessed August 2, 2012, http://
environment.alberta.ca/03183.html.

43 Government of Alberta, Alberta's Oil Sands, "Water," n.d.,
accessed February 12, 2012, www.oilsands.alberta.ca/water.
html; *see also*

Oil Sands Developers Group, "Oil Sands Environment
Fact Sheet" (October 2009): 7 ("Water"), PDF accessed
February 12, 2012, www.oilsandsdevelopers.ca/wp-content/
uploads/2009/06/Environment-Fact-Sheet-October-2009.
pdf.

God's Work

44 As quoted in Garth S. Jowett and Victoria O'Donnell, *Propaganda and Persuasion*, 4th ed. (Thousand Oaks, Calif.: Sage Publications Inc., 2006): 39.

45 Dale Lunan, "Rising Stars 2010," *Oilweek* 61, no. 5 (May 2010): 25, accessed May 30, 2012, through public library as specified in note 6, Canadian Business & Current Affairs Complete, ProQuest document ID 304192227.

46 Carrie Tait, "Saving the oil sands," *National Post*, August 21, 2010, accessed April 17, 2011, www.nationalpost.com/ Saving+sands/3424776/story.html.

47 Janet Annesley, "*Toxic Alberta* is mean-spirited and agenda-driven," CAPP, June 17, 2010, accessed April 16, 2011, http://is.gd/iZd32a.

48 US Chamber of Commerce, "About...," accessed February 28, 2012, www.uschamber.com/about.

49 *My Direct Democracy* group blog, "Tom Donahue, the 'Gang of 6' and Red America," posted December 13, 2006, by Matt Stoller, accessed May 30, 2012, http://mydd. com/2006/12/13/tom-donahue-the-gang-of-6-and-red-america; *see also*, as to the Chamber's 2010 budget:

    Eric Lipton, Mike McIntire and Don Van Natta Jr., "Top corporations aid U.S. Chamber of Commerce campaign," *New York Times*, October 21, 2010, accessed August 4, 2012, www.nytimes.com by searching for story title.

50 US Chamber of Commerce, "Climate Change," accessed July 15, 2012, www.uschamber.com/issues/environment/ climate-change.

51 American Petroleum Institute, "Membership," n.d., accessed June 21, 2012, www.api.org/globalitems/global-headerpages/membership.aspx.

52 Karen Matusic, "Canadian oil sands a boon to US economy, big job creator: Study," API, October 16, 2009, accessed June 21, 2012, http://is.gd/vajvYE.

53 Geoff Dembicki, "Oil sands lobbying without end, vows American Petroleum Institute," *The Tyee*, April 6, 2011, accessed June 21, 2012, http://is.gd/ETtYFa.

54 Jeff Gailus, "Mind Games," *Alberta Views* 12, no. 2, (March 2009): 33, accessed August 3, 2012, through public library as specified in note 6, Canadian Reference Centre (EBSCOHost) accession no. 36887816.

55 CAPP, Canada's Industry » Oil Sands » Environment, n.d., accessed August 4, 2012, www.capp.ca/canadaIndustry/oilSands/environment/Pages/default.aspx.

56 CAPP, "Canada's Industry » Oil Sands » Environment » Air » Greenhouse gas emissions," n.d., accessed June 21, 2012, http://is.gd/lwN9xV.

57 CAPP, "Video: Canada's Oil Sands – Come see for yourself," January 2010, Isaacs quote at ~10:45 in 15:46 flash video accessed June 21, 2012, http://is.gd/URloJ8.

58 Alberta Innovates, "Home," accessed July 15, 2012, www.ai-ees.ca/home/introduction.

59 CAPP, "Video: Canada's Oil Sands – Come see for yourself," as cited above in note 57, Newall quote at ~11:10; *see also* Newall variation of quote in:

Gary Park, "Techies lead the way," *Petroleum News* 10, no. 24, June 12, 2005, accessed June 21, 2012, www.petroleum-news.com/pntruncate/756742288.shtml.

60 Nikiforuk, *Tar Sands*, 128.

61 Responsible Canadian Energy [CAPP], The 2010 Report: How We Are Doing » Oil Sands » Air » "Greenhouse Gases," accessed February 26, 2012, www.rce2010.ca/oil-sands/air/greenhouse-gases; *see also*:

Joule A. Bergerson and David W. Keith, "The truth about dirty oil: Is CCS the answer?" *Environmental Science & Technology* 44, no. 16 (August 12, 2010): 6010–15, full text (HTML) accessed August 5, 2012, http://pubs.acs.org/doi/full/10.1021/es903812e.

62 Mark Evans, "The Republic of Bullshit: On the Dumbing-Up of Democracy," c. 12 in *Bullshit and Philosophy*, edited by Gary L. Hardcastle and George A. Reisch (Chicago: Open Court, 2006): 199.

63 Pembina Institute, OilSandsWatch.org, "Water Impacts," n.d., accessed July 15, 2012, www.pembina.org/oil-sands/os101/water.

64 Heather Douglas, "Bullshit at the Interface of Science and Policy: Global Warming, Toxic Substances and Other Pesky Problems," c. 14 in *Bullshit and Philosophy* as cited in note 62 above, 216.

65 Other good books about the use of bullshit by corporations include *Doubt Is Their Product*, by David Michaels; *Toxic Sludge Is Good for You!* by John Stauber and Sheldon Rampton; *Your Call Is Important to Us: The Truth about*

Bullshit, by Laura Penny; and *Climate Cover-Up*, by James Hoggan and Richard Littlemore.

66 "Smoking and Health Proposal" (1969): 4, in Brown & Williamson Collection, Legacy Tobacco Documents Library at University of California San Francisco, PDF of scanned typescript accessed April 19, 2011, http://legacy. library.ucsf.edu/tid/rgy93f00; *see also*, as to terms of the tobacco lawsuit settlement cited:

Scott Shane, "Tobacco firms agree to settle $368-billion penalty, to be paid out over 25 years," *Baltimore Sun*, June 21, 1997, accessed August 5, 2012, http://is.gd/hCn2cf.

67 Kevin Martin, "Alberta government claim alleges smoking industry conspiracy," *Calgary Sun*, June 11, 2012, accessed June 21, 2012, http://is.gd/dYCbNq.

68 Carrie Tait, "Saving the oil sands," as cited in note 46.

69 CAPP, Oil Sands » Dialogue & Resources » Public Opinion Research, "Canada–May 2010," PDF of PowerPoint-style bar graphs accessed February 26, 2012, http://is.gd/Yz6zCy.

70 CAPP, Upstream Dialogue, *The Facts on Oil Sands* (June 2012): 1 (PDF p3), accessed June 21, 2012, www.capp.ca/ UpstreamDialogue/OilSands/Pages/default.aspx.

71 CAPP, Environment & Community » Guiding Principles for Oil Sands Development » "Land," *Land Use in Canada's Oil Sands* (June 2012): 2, PDF accessed April 15, 2011, http://is.gd/gVH1eN.

72 Pembina Institute, OilSandsWatch.org, "Reclamation," n.d., accessed August 4, 2012, www.pembina.org/oil-sands/05101/reclamation; *see also,*

as to extent of disturbed lands in each stage of reclamation under Alberta's 2009 redefinitions:

Alberta Government, Alberta's Oil Sands » Alberta's Clean Energy Future » "Reclamation," accessed August 4, 2012, www.oilsands.alberta.ca/reclamation.html.

73 Natural Resources Canada, "Oil Sands: A strategic resource for Canada, North America and the global market" (August 2011): 4, PDF brochure accessed July 15, 2012, under title "Oil Sands – A strategic resource for Canada, North America and the world" from www.nrcan.gc.ca/energy/1167; *see also* note 77 below and

Alberta's Oil Sands, "Reclamation," accessed August 4, 2012, www.oilsands.alberta.ca/reclamation.html.

74 *Mining Works for Canada,* Special Edition Oil Sands vol. 1 (Summer 2007): 8, PDF accessed July 15, 2012, http://is.gd/qevW9C.

75 Mark Evans, "The Republic of Bullshit" as cited in note 62 above, 199.

76 *Rescuing the Frog* blog, "New Reclamation Guidelines (wonkish)," posted March 17, 2011, by Andrew Leach, accessed July 15, 2012, http://is.gd/Z69n9c.

77 Conservation and Reclamation Regulation, Alta. Reg. 115/93, ss. 1(*e*), 2, accessed July 15, 2012, http://canlii.ca/t/lfxb.

78 Barry Robinson, "Well Abandonment and Reclamation in Alberta: The Failure of the Licensee Liability Rating Program," prepared for the Canadian Institute's Well and Pipeline Abandonment, Suspension and Reclamation Conference, February 9–10, 2010, PDF accessed July 15, 2012, www.ecojustice.ca/publications/well-abandonment-and-reclamation-in-alberta.

79 CAPP, "Advertising Standards Canada rules CAPP ad not misleading," press release, November 30, 2010, accessed August 4, 2012, http://is.gd/5MnW7d; *see also* note 10 above and YouTube at http://is.gd/LYjJ7X.

80 Sierra Club Canada, "CAPP withdraws yogurt ad in response to Sierra Club Canada complaint," press release, November 30, 2010, accessed April 14, 2011, www.sierraclub.ca/en/node/3470; *see also*

Advertising Standards Canada, "The 14 Clauses of the Canadian Code of Advertising Standards," www.adstandards.com/en/standards/the14Clauses.aspx.

81 CAPP, as cited above in note 79.

82 Carol Christian, "Ad criticized for comparing tailings to yogurt," *Fort McMurray Today*, n.d., accessed April 18, 2011, http://is.gd/HKLRfL.

83 Nathan Vanderklippe, "Oil patch yogurt ad not misleading, council says," *Globe and Mail*, November 30 2010, accessed August 1, 2012, http://is.gd/5dH5Ru.

84 CAPP and YouTube, as cited above in note 79.

85 John Vidal, "Shell rapped by ASA for 'greenwash' advert," *The Guardian*, August 13, 2008, accessed July 15, 2012, http://is.gd/BWtAKm.

86 Martin Hickman, "Shell rebuked for 'greenwash' over ad for polluting oil project," *The Independent*, August 13, 2008, accessed April 17, 2011, http://is.gd/XQJSEx.

87 Vidal, "Shell rapped by ASA…" as cited above in note 85.

88 Alan Richardson, "Performing Bullshit and the Post-Sincere Condition," c. 6 in *Bullshit and Philosophy* as cited in note 62 above, 93–94.

89 *Tipping Point* documentary as cited in note 33, at ~27:35.

90 Tzeporah Berman, "'Ethical oil' campaign polluting our children's minds," *Huffington Post Canada*, October 21, 2011, accessed May 30, 2012, http://is.gd/u02ywa.

91 Office of the Auditor General of Canada, *2011 October Report of the Commissioner of the Environment and Sustainable Development*, "The Commissioner's Perspective," full text (HTML) accessed July 15, 2012, http://is.gd/T6hwSo.

Breaking All the Rules

92 Environment Canada, "Notes for Remarks by The Honourable Peter Kent, PC, MP, Minister of the Environment, Calgary Chamber of Commerce, January, 26, 2012," accessed May 30, 2012, http://is.gd/UmXcHU.

93 Nick Snow, "Watching government: Alberta Premier's outlook," *Oil & Gas Journal*, March 19, 2012, preview accessed May 30, 2012, http://is.gd/uAigfC.

94 David R. Boyd, "Little green lies: Prime Minister Harper and Canada's environment," *iPolitics*, February 8, 2012, accessed May 30, 2012, http://is.gd/baZW5a.

95 Ibid.

96 Office of the Auditor General of Canada, *2011 October Report of the Commissioner of the Environment and Sustainable Development*, "Chapter 2: Assessing Cumulative Environmental Effects of Oil Sands Projects," §2.3 "Environmental assessment of projects," full text (HTML) accessed May 30, 2012, http://is.gd/cwvUKx.

97 William Leiss, "How Canada's Stumbles with Environmental Risk Management Reflect an Integrity Gap," c. 2 in *The Integrity Gap: Canada's Environmental Policy and Institutions*, edited by Eugene Lee and Anthony Perl (Vancouver: UBC Press, 2003): 30.

98 Steve Hrudey et al., *Environmental and Health Impacts of Canada's Oil Sands Industry* (Ottawa: Royal Society of Canada, December 2010): 280 (PDF p304), accessed August 2, 2012, at www.rsc.ca/creports.php; *see also*, as to quotes in the next paragraph in the text:

Canadian Environmental Assessment Act, S.C. 1992, c 37, Preamble and s. 4(1)(*a*), full text (HTML) accessed March 2, 2012, http://canlii.ca/t/kwcj [stable link to version that was current at time accessed];

NB: while this book was in production, the 1992 Act was repealed and replaced by the Canadian Environmental Assessment Act, 2012, S.C. 2012, c. 19, s. 52, http://canlii.ca/t/51w48, proclaimed in force July 6, 2012, Canada

Gazette Pt. II, SI/2012-56, http://is.gd/BRbF5D, both accessed August 15, 2012.

99 Office of the Auditor General of Canada, *2011 October Report*, c. 2, as cited above in note 96, §2.19.

100 Ibid., §§2.20, 2.25.

101 Federal Court of Canada, *Pembina Institute v. Canada (Attorney General)*, 2008 FC 302 (March 5, 2008), ¶¶17ff, 50ff, full text accessed August 2, 2012, http://is.gd/w1Zp37.

102 *ABlawg.ca* (University of Calgary Faculty of Law blog), "Back on track to socio-ecological ruin: Kearl oil sands project re-authorized," posted June 16, 2008, by Shawn Fluker, accessed May 30, 2012, http://is.gd/53Wiib; *see also,* in a linked March 26, 2008, post by Fluker, "Just a bump on the road to socio-ecological ruin...," the following:

> "The law/policy dualism that permeates judicial and regulatory decision-making with respect to energy projects and their socio-ecological impacts allows the judiciary and regulators such as the ERCB to avoid addressing the concerns of those affected by these projects, by simply categorizing them as policy matters."

103 As detailed in Arlene J. Kwasniak, "Use and abuse of adaptive management in environmental assessment law and practice: A Canadian example and general lessons," *Journal of Environmental Assessment Policy & Management* 12, no. 4 (December 2010): 425–68, full text (PDF) accessed August 3, 2012, through http://calgarypubliclibrary.com/books-more/e-library?s=88, Environment Complete (EBSCOHost) accession no. 57872088.

104 Alberta Environment, *Guideline for Wetland Establishment on Reclaimed Oil Sands Leases*, revised ed. (2007): 86 and passim, PDF accessed August 5, 2012, environment.gov.ab.ca/info/library/8105.pdf;

D.W. Schindler and W.F. Donahue, "An impending water crisis in Canada's western prairie provinces," *Proceedings of the National Academy of Sciences* 103, no. 19 (May 9, 2006): 7210–16, full text (HTML) accessed August 5, 2012, www.pnas.org/content/103/19/7210.full; *see also*

Rebecca C. Rooney et al., "Oil sands mining and reclamation cause massive loss of peatland and stored carbon," *PNAS* 109, no. 13 (March 27, 2012): 4933–37, full text, same access date, www.pnas.org/content/109/13/4933.full.

105 Alberta Environment, *Provincial Wetland Restoration/ Compensation Guide* (rev. ed. 2007): 7 (PDF p12), accessed August 5, 2012, http://environment.alberta.ca/01126.html.

106 Kwasniak, as cited in note 103 above, 447.

107 Fay Westcott and Lindsay Watson, *End Pit Lakes Technical Guidance Document*, prepared for CEMA (Fort McMurray, Alta.: March 2007): 4 (PDF p18), accessed July 15, 2012, www.ceaa.gc.ca/050/documents_staticpost/cearref_37519/44851/t.pdf.

108 *Pembina Institute v. Canada (Attorney General)* as cited in note 101 above, ¶56.

109 Ibid., ¶78; *cf also* the *ABLawg* posts cited in note 102.

110 Office of the Auditor General of Canada, *2011 October Report*, c. 2, as cited in note 96 above, §2.30.

111 Ibid.

112 William Leiss, personal correspondence with the author, February 7, 2012.

113 Peter O'Neil, "Second former Tory minister blasts plan for Fisheries Act," *Edmonton Journal*, March 21, 2012, accessed August 2, 2012, through public library as specified in note 6, Canadian Newsstand, ProQuest document ID 938016507; *see also*, as to polls, e.g.:

Nature Canada, "Canadians oppose turning lakes into dumps, even at expense of jobs, according to national poll," press release April 12, 2012, accessed August 2, 2012, naturecanada.ca/newsroom_apr_12_12_water.asp;

Ipsos Reid, "One half (52%) of small business owners are going green," header accessed August 2, 2012, http://is.gd/eBMohK;

Christopher Majka, "The turning tide: Canadians and our energy future," re July 2012 Harris-Decima poll for Tides Canada, accessed August 2, 2012, http://is.gd/1ptESR.

114 Jason Fekete, "Oil, gas reviews to be reined in," *Edmonton Journal*, March 30, 2012, accessed August 2, 2012, through public library as specified in note 6, Canadian Newsstand, ProQuest document ID 963600115; *cf*, as to CEAA changes, the latter two-thirds of note 98.

115 Rebecca Lindell, "New environmental review rules to apply retroactively," Global News, March 30, 2012, accessed May 30, 2012, http://is.gd/aCfwal.

116 Richard Lindgren, personal communication with the author, March 20, 2012.

117 Geoff Dembicki, "Canada teams with oil lobby to fight US clean energy clause," *The Tyee*, March 16, 2011, accessed April 6, 2011, http://is.gd/3WRvRt.

118 Dembicki, "Killer of US clean energy laws now running for Alberta premier," *The Tyee*, April 5, 2011, http://thetyee.ca/News/2011/04/05/GaryMar.

119 Gary Mar, "Why Gary?" Mar Alberta Conservative Party leadership campaign, July 6, 2011, accessed August 5, 2012, through the Wayback Machine, http://wayback.archive.org/web/*/http://www.garymar.ca/gary/* [the two "wildcard" asterisks are necessary parts of this URL].

120 Dembicki as cited above in note 118.

121 Dembicki, "Climate group says Washington's oil sands war is 'David vs. Goliath,'" *The Tyee*, March 28, 2011, accessed April 6, 2011, http://is.gd/3AQXmg.

122 Sheldon Alberts, "Mr. Doer goes to Washington: Well-connected," *National Post*, October 19, 2009, A5, accessed August 5, 2012, through public library as specified in note 6, Canadian Newsstand, ProQuest document ID 330867179.

123 Climate Action Network Canada, "New report reveals Canadian efforts to kill climate change policies in other countries," press release November 22, 2010, accessed July 15, 2012, http://is.gd/cpGvU7.

124 Stanley Tromp, "Canada lobbied US over TransCanada's Keystone pipeline," *Financial Post*, January 23, 2011, accessed June 22, 2012, http://is.gd/3N9cyC.

125 Carl Meyer, "Canada's high-powered energy advocates," *Embassy*, August 4, 2010, accessed August 10, 2012, http://is.gd/IMiZl2.

126 Climate Action Network Canada, Kevin Stringer, Director General, Petroleum Resources Branch, to Philip Owen, Head of Unit, Environment Directorate-General, September 24, 2009, PDF [cached] accessed August 5, 2012, http://is.gd/3VlhpF.

127 Dembicki, "Why Europe could decide fate of Canada's oil sands," *The Tyee*, October 20, 2010, accessed July 15, 2012, http://thetyee.ca/News/2010/10/20/EuropeDecidesFate; *see also*, for link to Brandt paper mentioned in next paragraph in the text:

Transport & Environment [NGO], "Report for Commission confirms carbon-intensity of tar sands," February 11, 2011, accessed August 5, 2012, http://is.gd/OXWzsQ.

128 Damian Carrington, "EU tar sands pollution vote ends in deadlock," *The Guardian*, February 23, 2012, accessed May 30, 2012, http://is.gd/VnrFJ1.

129 Michael A. Levi, *The Canadian Oil Sands: Energy Security vs. Climate Change* (New York: Council on Foreign Relations Press, 2009): 22. *see also*, as to current US domestic oil production,

Neela Banerjee, "US report: Oil imports down, domestic production highest since 2003," *Los Angeles Times*, March 12, 2012, http://is.gd/qsIg1T.

130 Neil S. Swart and Andrew Weaver, "The Alberta oil sands and climate," *Nature Climate Change* 2, no. 3 (March 2012,

print): 134–36, citation accessed May 30, 2012, http://is.gd/
XO80BV.

131 Nathan Vanderklippe, "Oil sands proponents get a PR
     boost," *Globe and Mail*, February 21, 2012, accessed March
     6, 2012, http://is.gd/PvmBTy.

132 Vanderklippe, "Canada's oil sands: not so dirty after all,"
     Globe and Mail, February 20, 2012, accessed March 6, 2012,
     http://is.gd/mPxmOC.

133 Andrew Weaver, "The oilsands are a symptom of the bigger
     problem of our dependence on fossil fuels," *Toronto Star*,
     February 21, 2012, accessed August 10, 2012, http://is.gd/
     mXfzoH.

134 Mark Jaccard, "You can't take the tar sands out of the
     climate equation," *Globe and Mail*, February 28, 2012,
     accessed March 6, 2012, http://is.gd/rtmF7n.

135 International Energy Agency, *World Energy Outlook
     2009* (Paris): 44 (PDF p46) accessed March 6, 2012, www.
     worldenergyoutlook.org/publications/weo-2009.

Rethinking Advocacy

136 Michael Marx, personal communication with the author,
     March 30, 2011.

137 Corporate Ethics International, accessed May 7, 2011,
     http://corpethics.org.

138 Richard Blackwell, "Neither sellouts nor 'wing-nut tree-
     huggers,'" *Globe and Mail*, April 4, 2011, accessed August 4,
     2012, http://is.gd/QtJoZX.

139 *Language Matters* blog, "Sharing the road," posted
February 28, 2011, by Peter McKenzie-Brown, accessed
April 15, 2011, http://languageinstinct.blogspot.
com/2011/02/sharing-road.html; also appeared in *Oilweek*
62, no. 3 (March 2011): 60–62, accessed August 2, 2012,
through public library as specified in note 6, Canadian
Business & Current Affairs Complete, ProQuest document ID 854504518.

140 Michael Marx, personal communication with the author,
March 30, 2011.

141 Ziva Kunda, "The case for motivated reasoning,"
Psychological Bulletin 108, no. 3 (1990): 480–98, PDF scan
accessed August 5, 2012, http://cogsci.uwaterloo.ca/ziva/
psychbul1990.pdf.

142 Tim Dickinson, "The Climate Killers," *Rolling Stone*
(January 6, 2010): 12, "The Coal Baron," accessed August 4,
2012, through the Wayback Machine, http://web.archive.
org/web/20100111034022/http://www.rollingstone.com/
politics/story/31633524/the_climate_killers/12.

143 Christopher Joyce, "Belief in climate change hinges on
worldview," National Public Radio, February 23, 2010,
accessed May 30, 2012, www.npr.org/templates/story/story.
php?storyId=124008307.

144 Ibid.

145 Ibid.

146 Michael Marx, personal communication with the author,
March 30, 2011.

147 Ibid.

148 Jeff Wells et al., *Danger in the Nursery: Impact on Birds of Tar Sands Oil Development in Canada's Boreal Forest* (New York: Natural Resources Defense Council, 2008), PDF accessed August 5, 2012, www.nrdc.org/wildlife/borealbirds.asp.

149 Kevin Timoney, "Toll of oilsands tailings ponds on migratory birds is difficult to measure," *Edmonton Journal* op-ed, December 9, 2008, A10, accessed through public library as specified in note 6, Canadian Newsstand, ProQuest document ID 250680346.

150 Kevin Timoney and Robert Ronconi, "Annual bird mortality in the bitumen tailings ponds in northeastern Alberta, Canada," *The Wilson Journal of Ornithology* 122, no. 3 (September 2010): 569–76, abstract and references accessed September 5, 2012, www.bioone.org/doi/abs/10.1676/09-181.1.

151 Jodie Sinnema, "Bird death totals don't add up: Study," canada.com, September 7, 2010, accessed June 22, 2012, http://is.gd/OkjKLW.

152 Mark Evans, "The Republic of Bullshit" as cited in note 62 above, 199.

153 "Alberta oilsands battles blackened reputation," *Energize Alberta*, December 5, 2011, accessed May 30, 2012, http://is.gd/MgSDbv.

154 Michael Marx, personal communication with the author, March 30, 2011.

155 Meagan Fitzpatrick, "Oilsands 'allies' and 'adversaries' named in federal documents," CBC News, January 26, 2012, accessed July 15, 2012, http://is.gd/uvRo4l.

156 Natural Resources Canada, "An open letter from
The Honourable Joe Oliver etc.," January 9, 2012,
accessed July 15, 2012, www.nrcan.gc.ca/media-room/
news-release/2012/1/3520.

157 Andrew Frank, In the media » Whistleblower, "1st
Affidavit of Andrew Frank," January 23, 2012, PDF accessed
July 15, 2012, http://andrewfrank.ca/in-the-media/
whistleblower; *see also*, as to Gingrich memo mentioned in
next paragraph in text:

"'Language: A key mechanism of control,'" Fairness &
Accuracy in Reporting, February 1995, accessed August 4,
2012, www.fair.org/index.php?page=1276.

158 "Jonathan Haidt explains our contentious culture," Moyers
& Company interview February 3, 2012, video (47:09) and
full transcript accessed August 4, 2012, http://is.gd/yOc5ao.

159 Alan Broadbent, "Pipeline politics: Don't demonize
the charitable sector," *Globe and Mail*, January 12, 2012,
accessed July 15, 2012, http://is.gd/A8CZPs.

160 "Waste makes haste: Eco-pests force government to
streamline hearings," *Calgary Herald* editorial, January 28,
2012, A14, accessed August 6, 2012, through public library
as specified in note 6, Canadian Newsstand, ProQuest
document ID 918717473.

161 Robert Gibson, "Bullshit," *Alternatives Journal* 37, no.
1 (January 2011): 40, accessed August 5, 2012, www.
alternativesjournal.ca/node/880.

162 *GreenPolicyProf* blog, "The three logics of climate politics,"
posted February 13, 2012, by George Hoberg, accessed June
22, 2012, http://is.gd/iMBWQe.

Other Titles in this Series

Digging the City

An Urban Agriculture Manifesto

Rhona McAdam

ISBN 978-1-927330-21-0

Gift Ecology

Reimagining a Sustainable World

Peter Denton

ISBN 978-1-927330-40-1

The Insatiable Bark Beetle

Dr. Reese Halter

ISBN 978-1-926855-67-7

The Incomparable Honeybee

and the Economics of Pollination
Revised & Updated

Dr. Reese Halter

ISBN 978-1-926855-65-3

The Beaver Manifesto

Glynnis Hood

ISBN 978-1-926855-58-5

The Grizzly Manifesto

In Defence of the Great Bear

by Jeff Gailus

ISBN 978-1-897522-83-7

Becoming Water

Glaciers in a Warming World

Mike Demuth

ISBN 978-1-926855-72-1

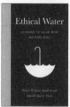

Ethical Water

Learning To Value What Matters Most

Robert William Sandford
& Merrell-Ann S. Phare

ISBN 978-1-926855-70-7

Denying the Source

The Crisis of First Nations Water Rights

Merrell-Ann S. Phare

ISBN 978-1-897522-61-5

The Weekender Effect

Hyperdevelopment in Mountain Towns

Robert William Sandford

ISBN 978-1-897522-10-3

RMB saved the following resources by printing
the pages of this book on chlorine-free paper
made with 100% post-consumer waste:

Trees · 9, fully grown

Water · 4,207 gallons

Energy · 4 million BTUs

Solid Waste · 282 pounds

Greenhouse Gases · 775 pounds

Calculations based on research by Environmental Defense and
the Paper Task Force. Manufactured at Friesens Corporation.